Hi and thank you for choosing my book.

It's my priority to continue providing top-notch books to customers like you.

Please leave me a review.

It will only take a minute, but it will make a huge difference for my work.

Thanks again!

Colored By:

_____

Date:_____

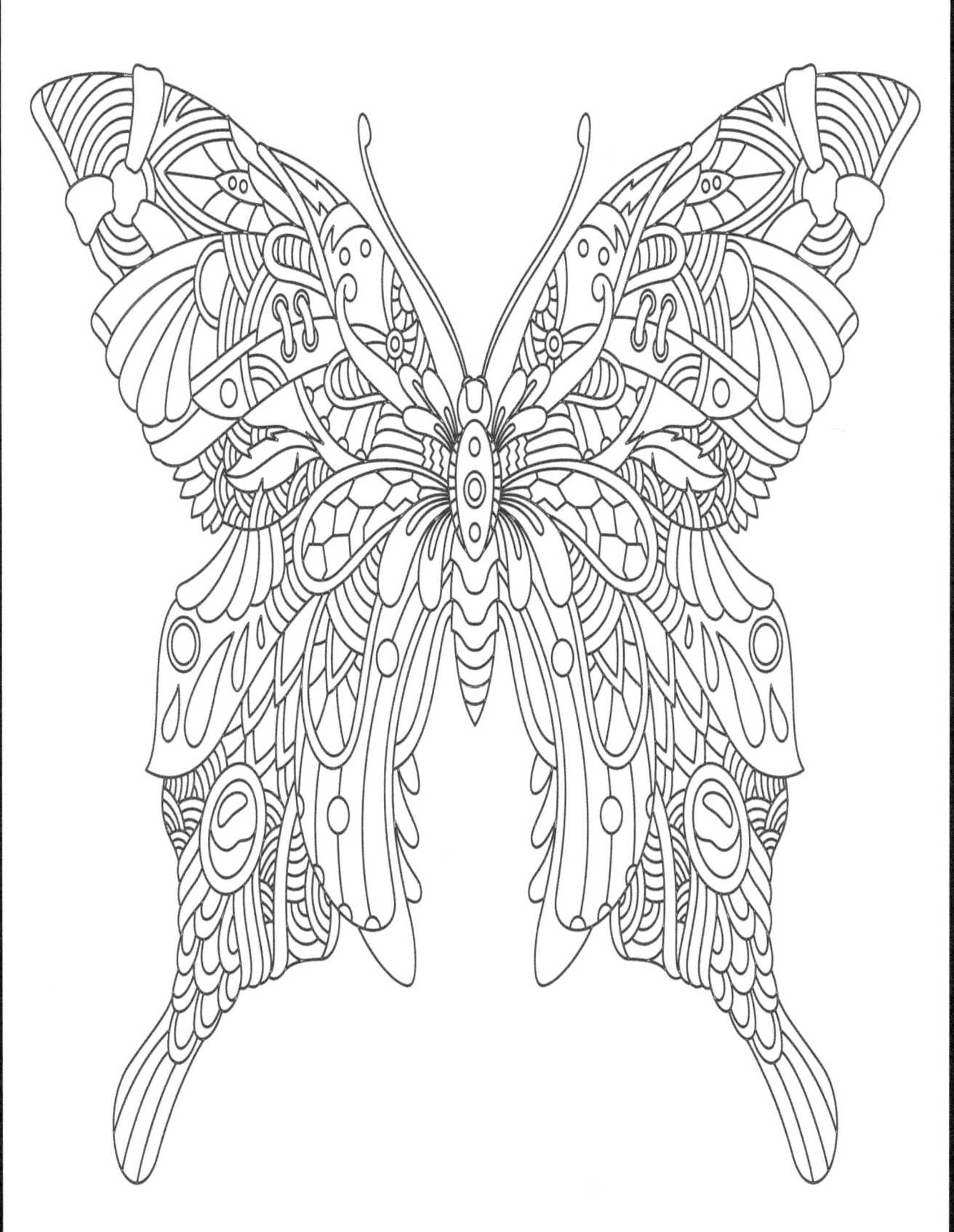

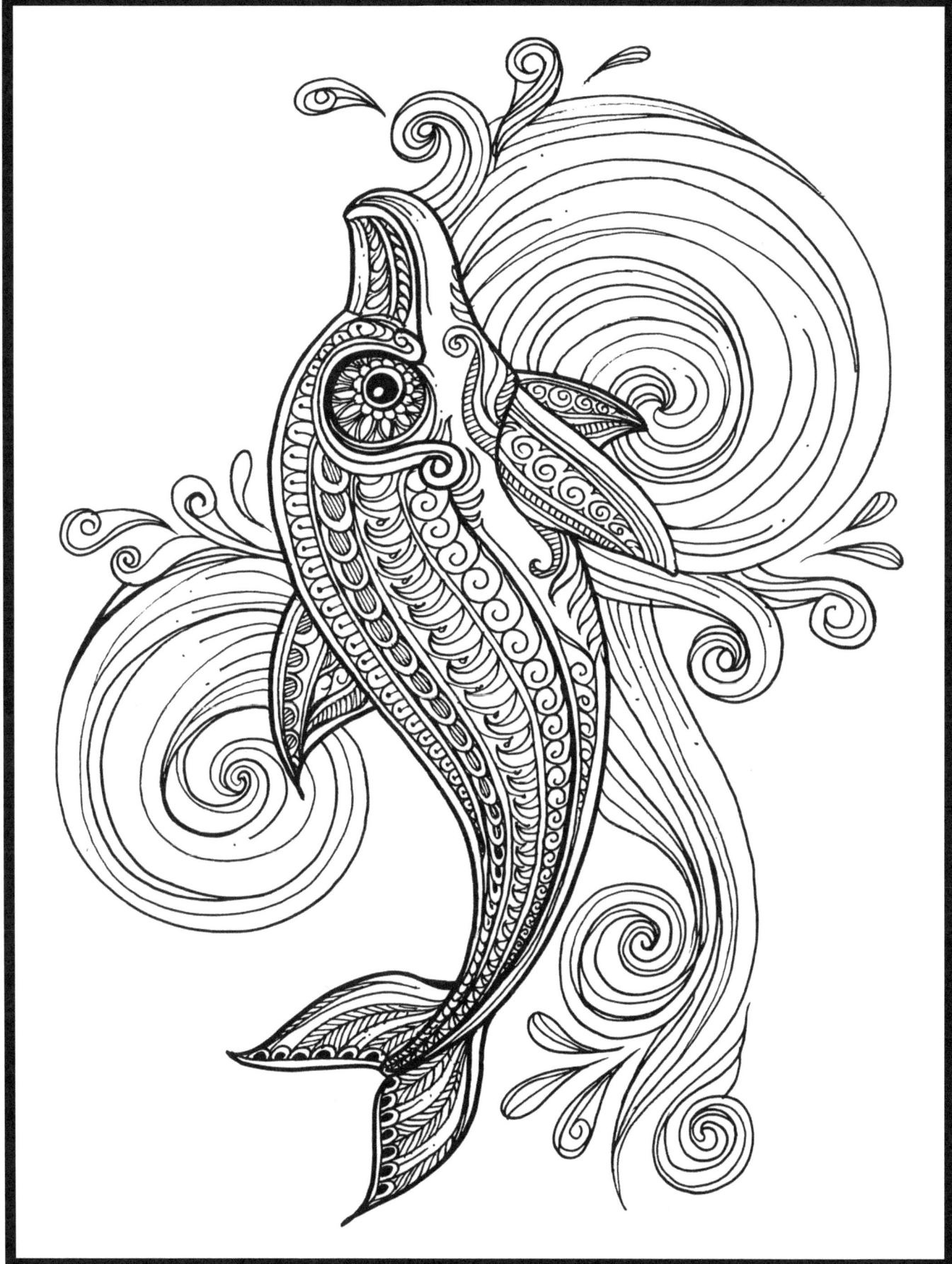

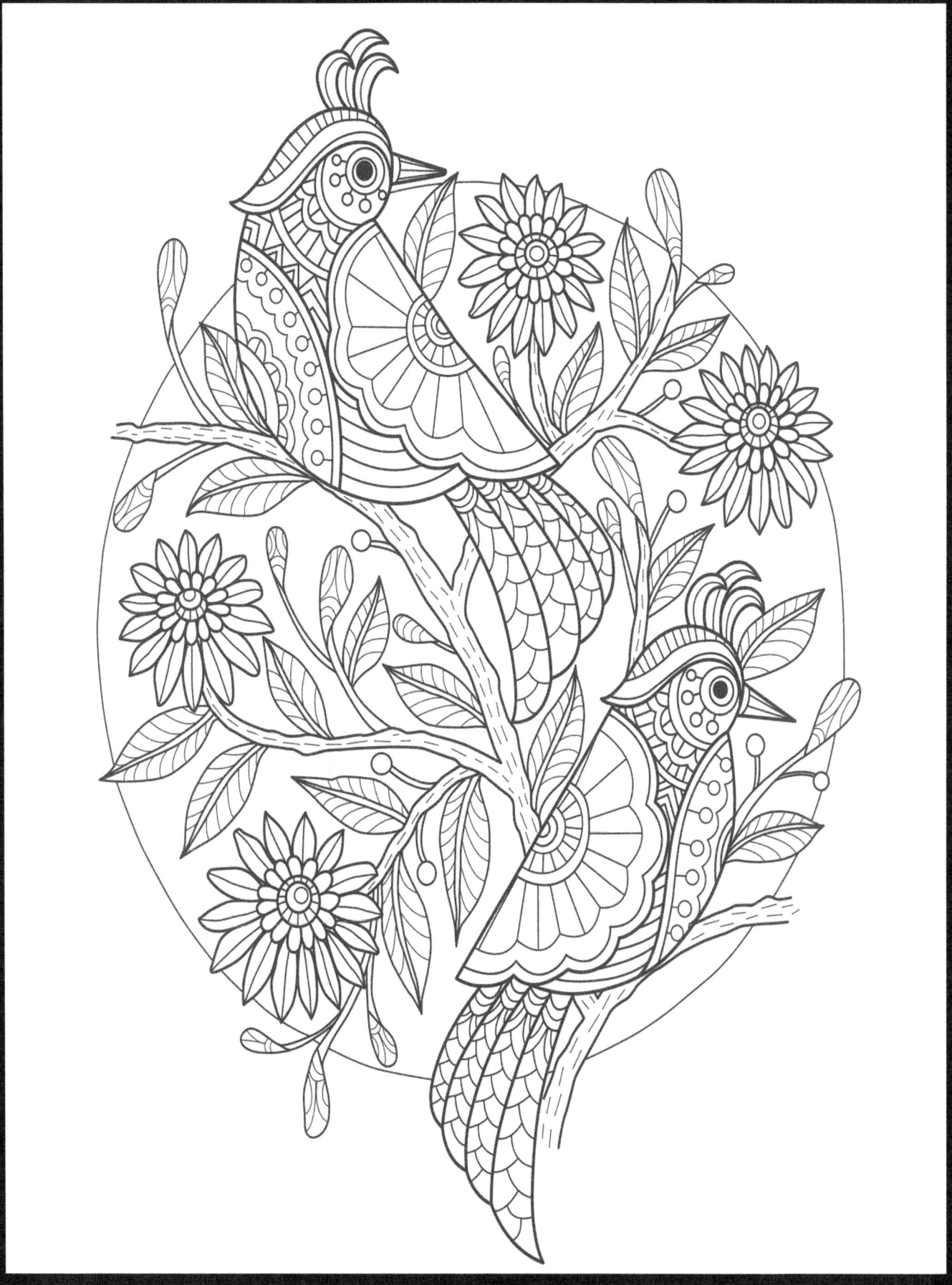

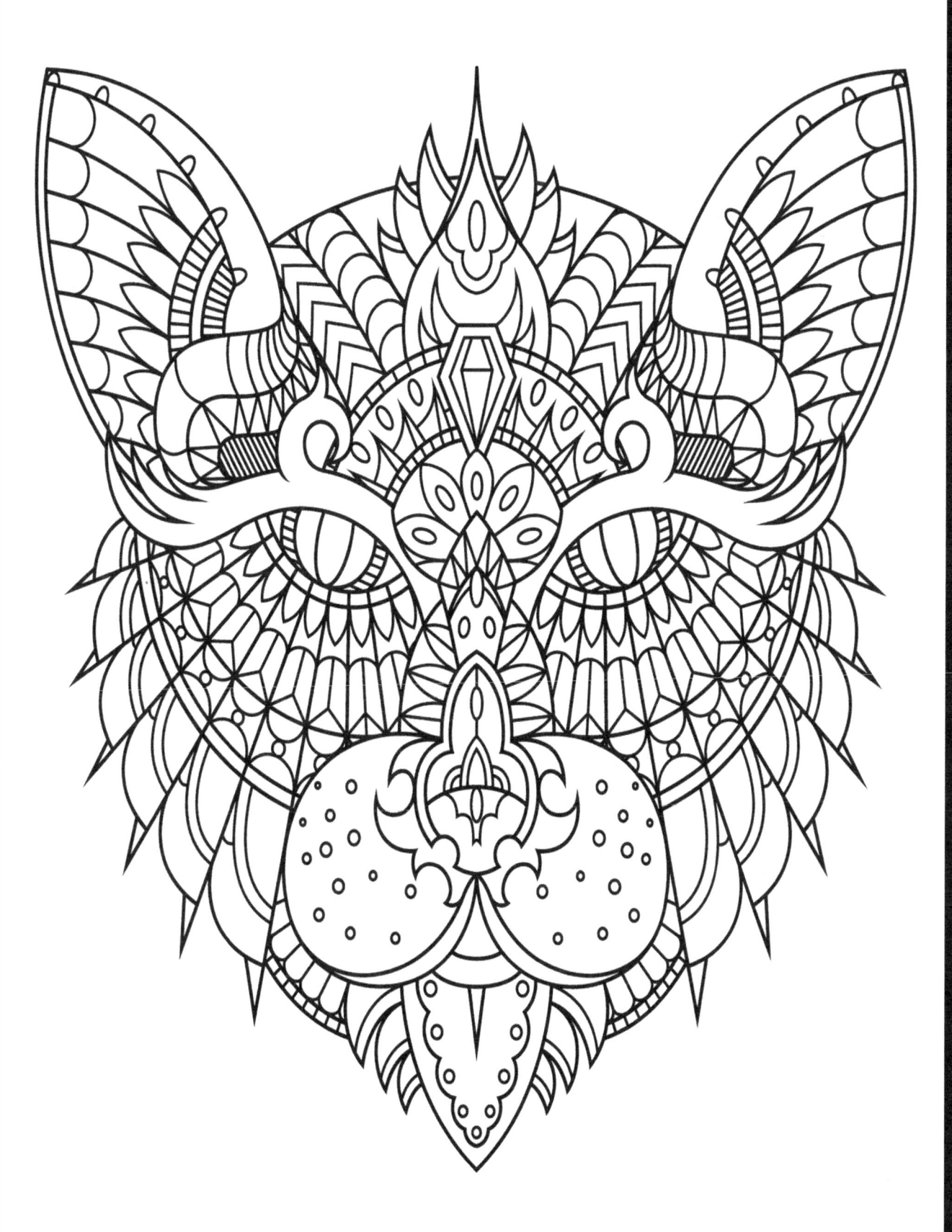

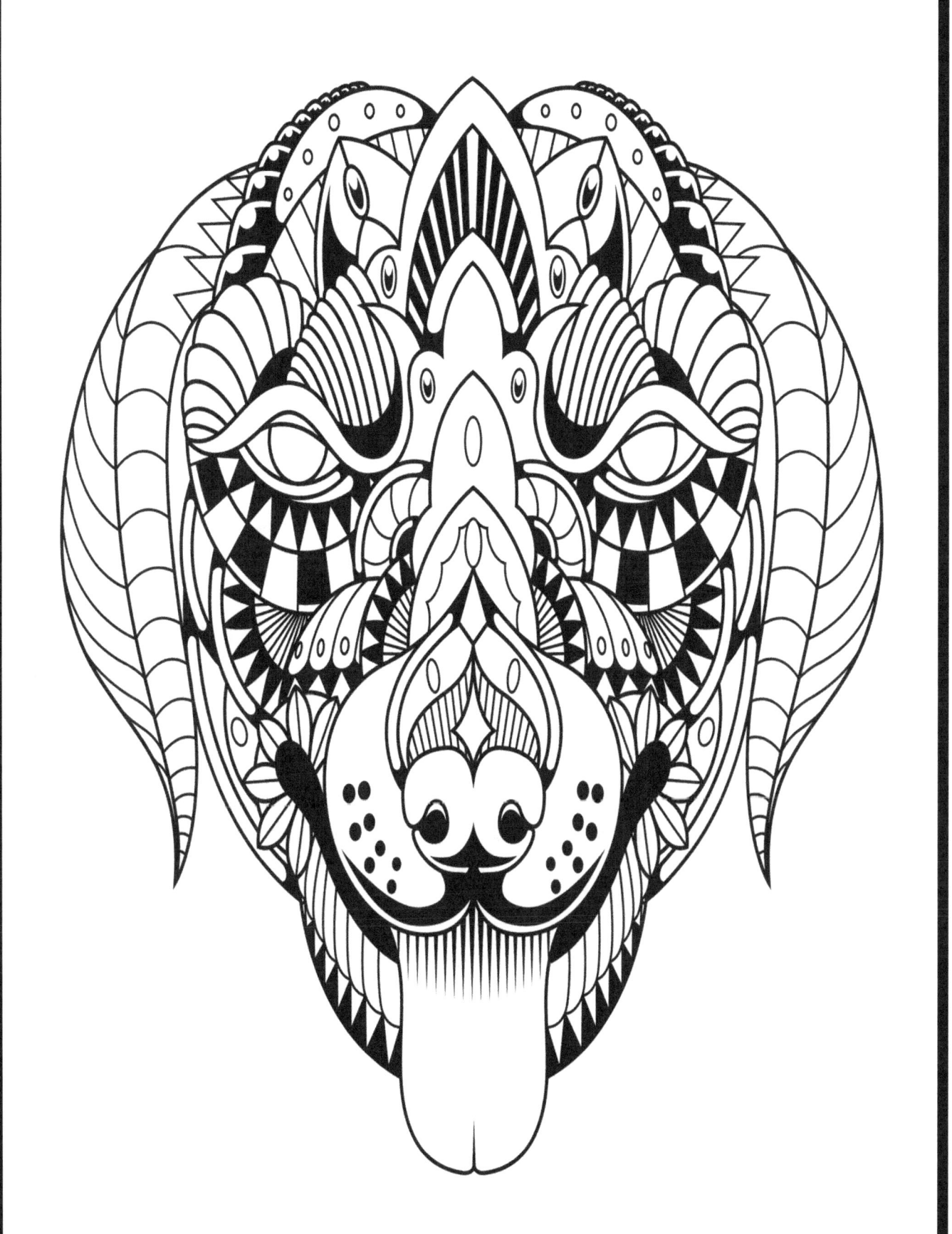

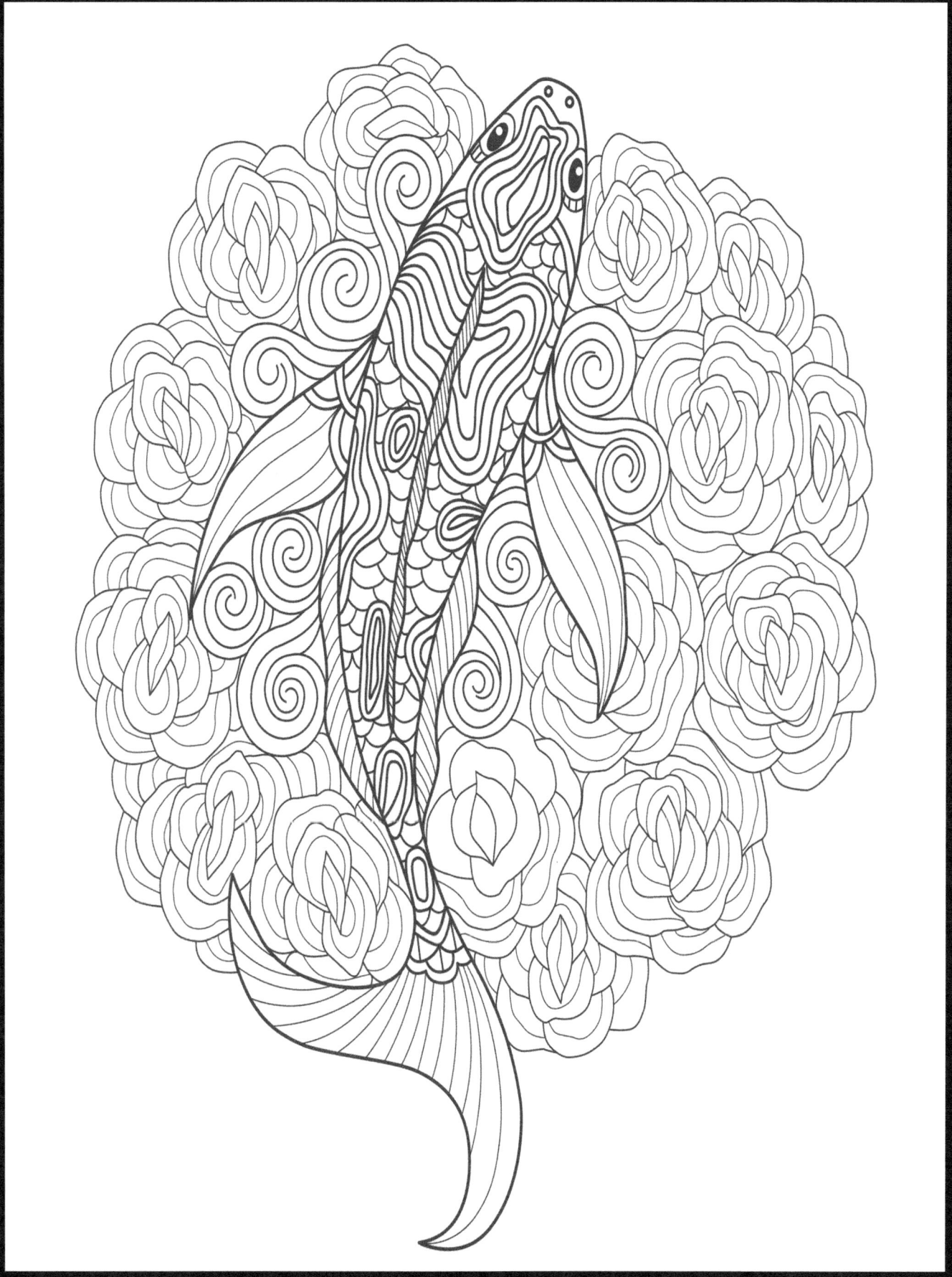

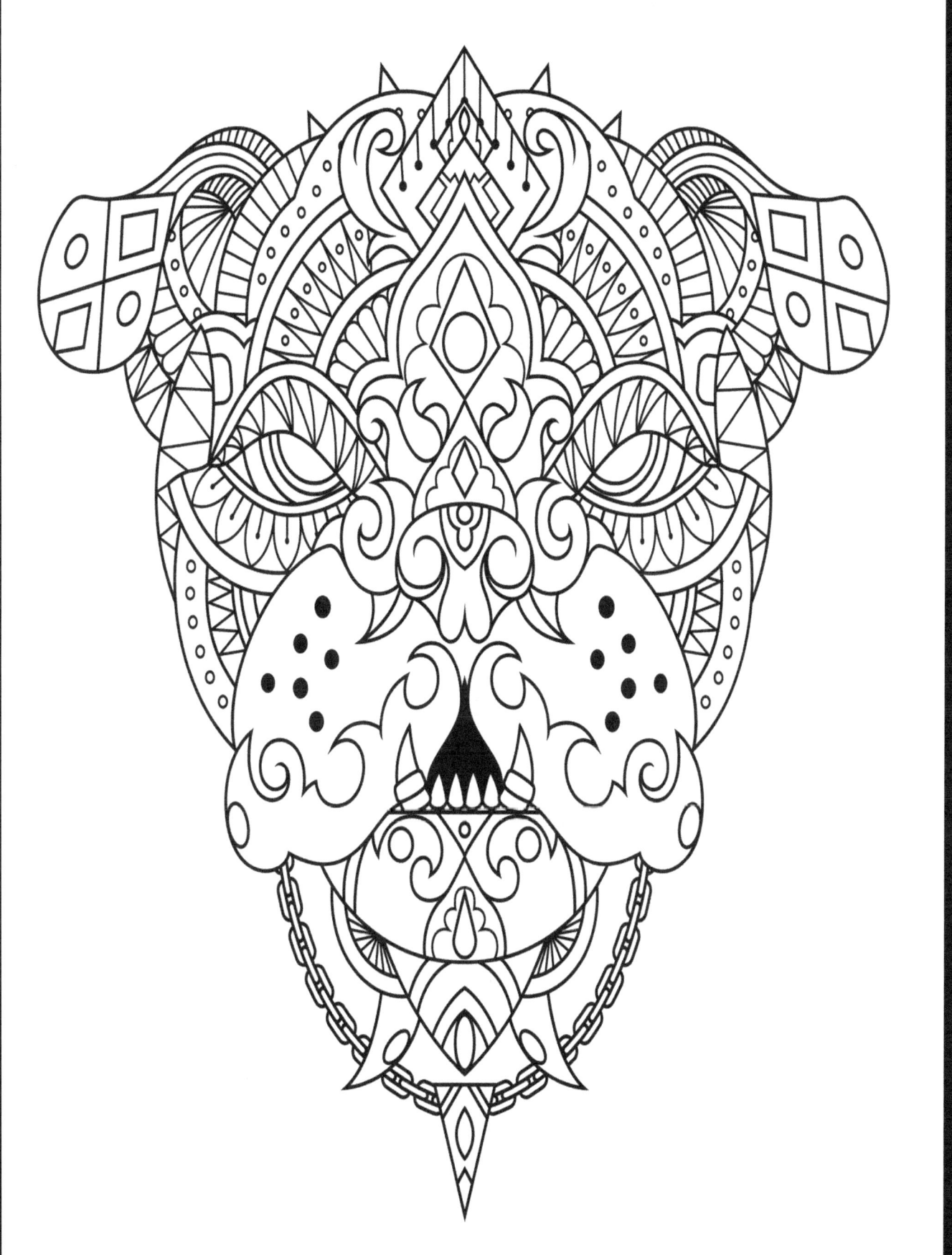

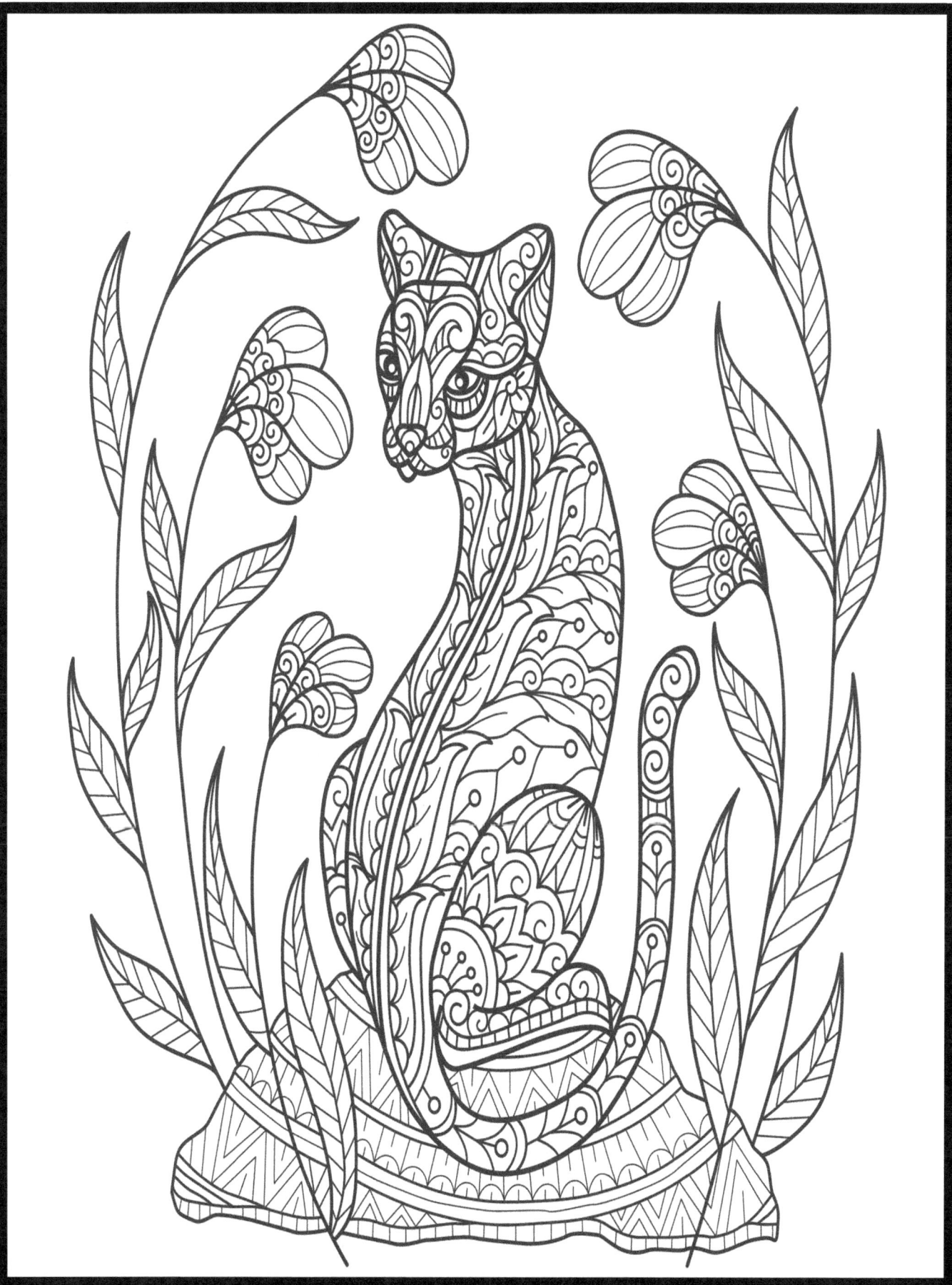

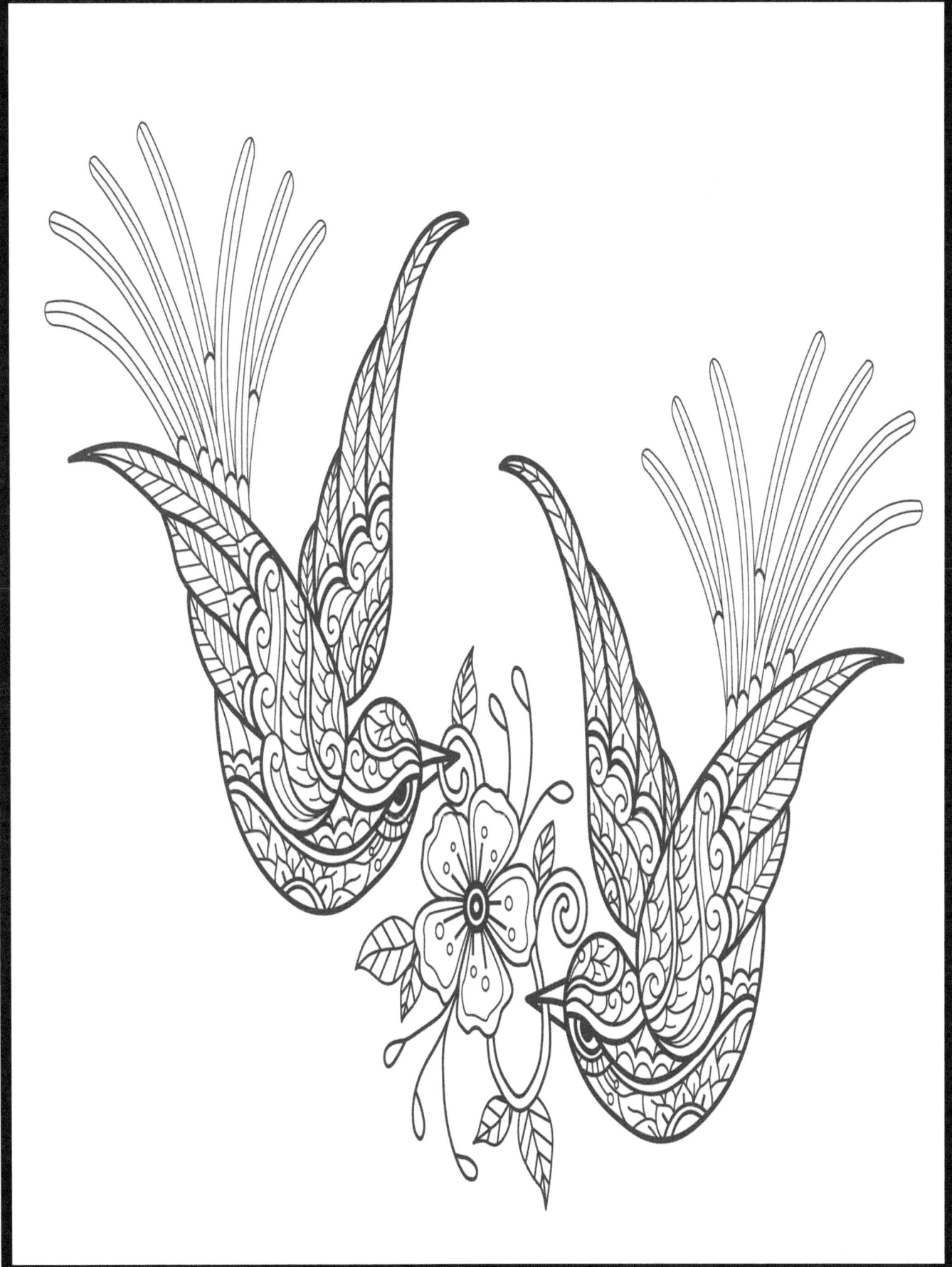

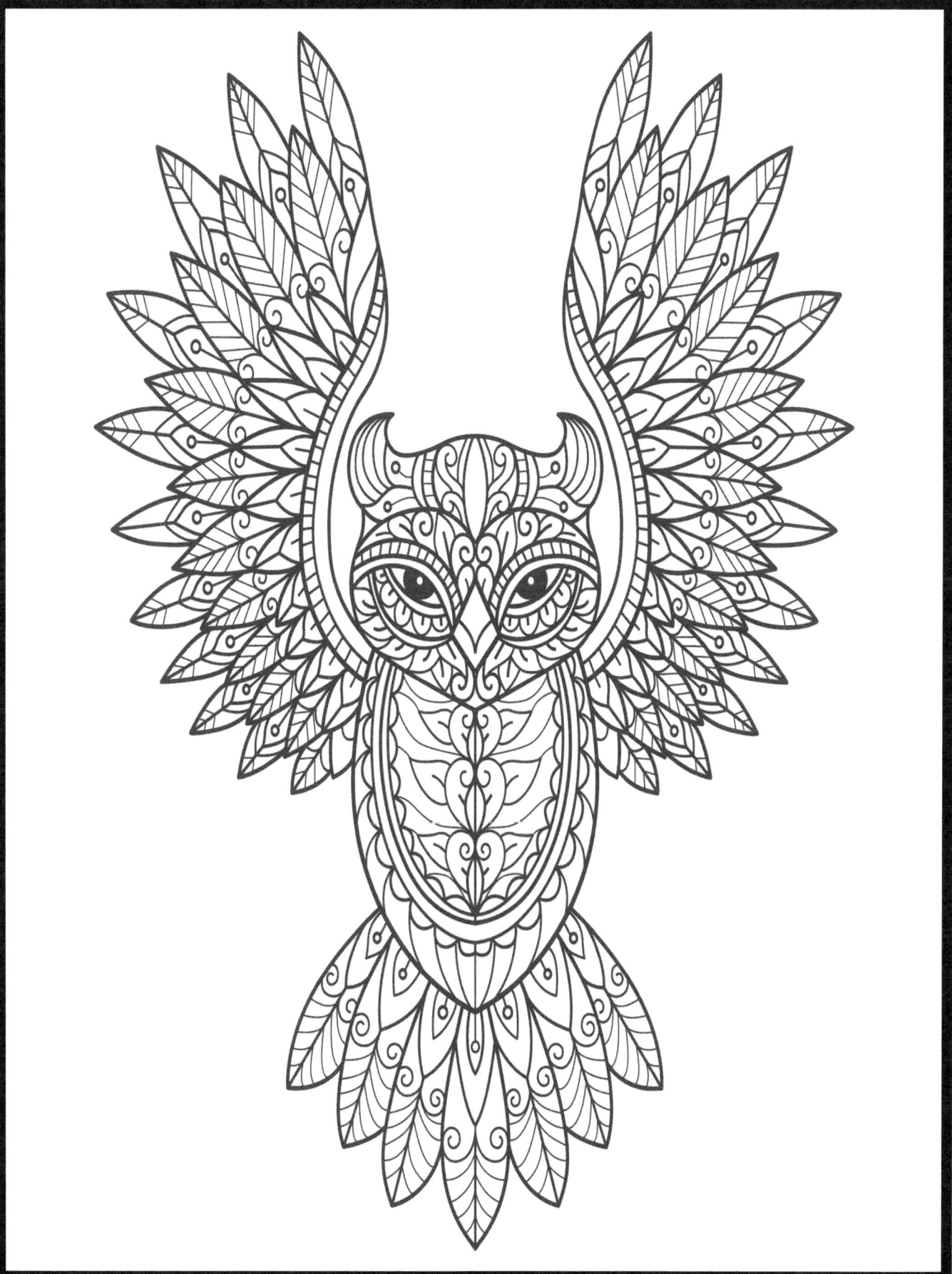

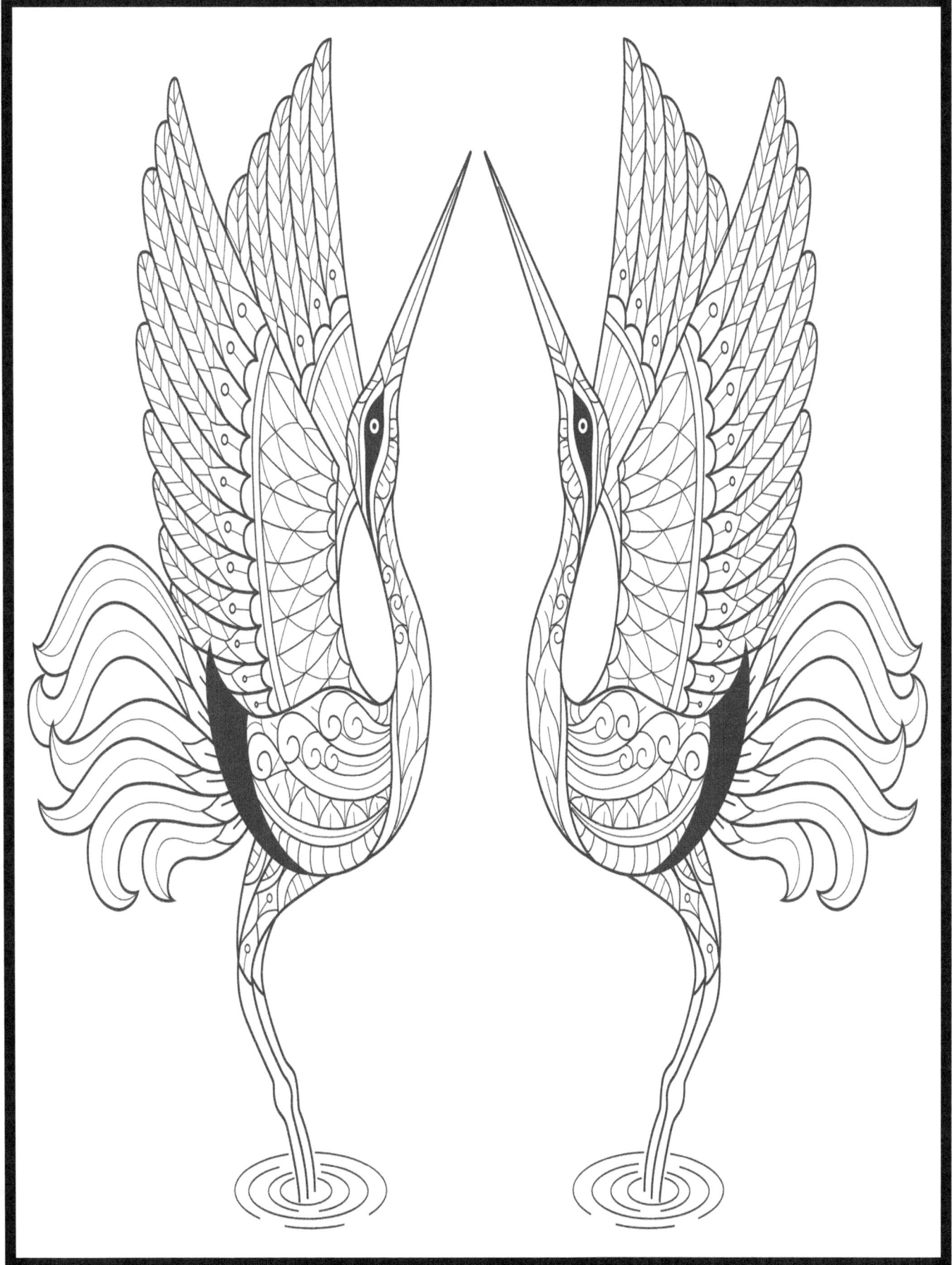

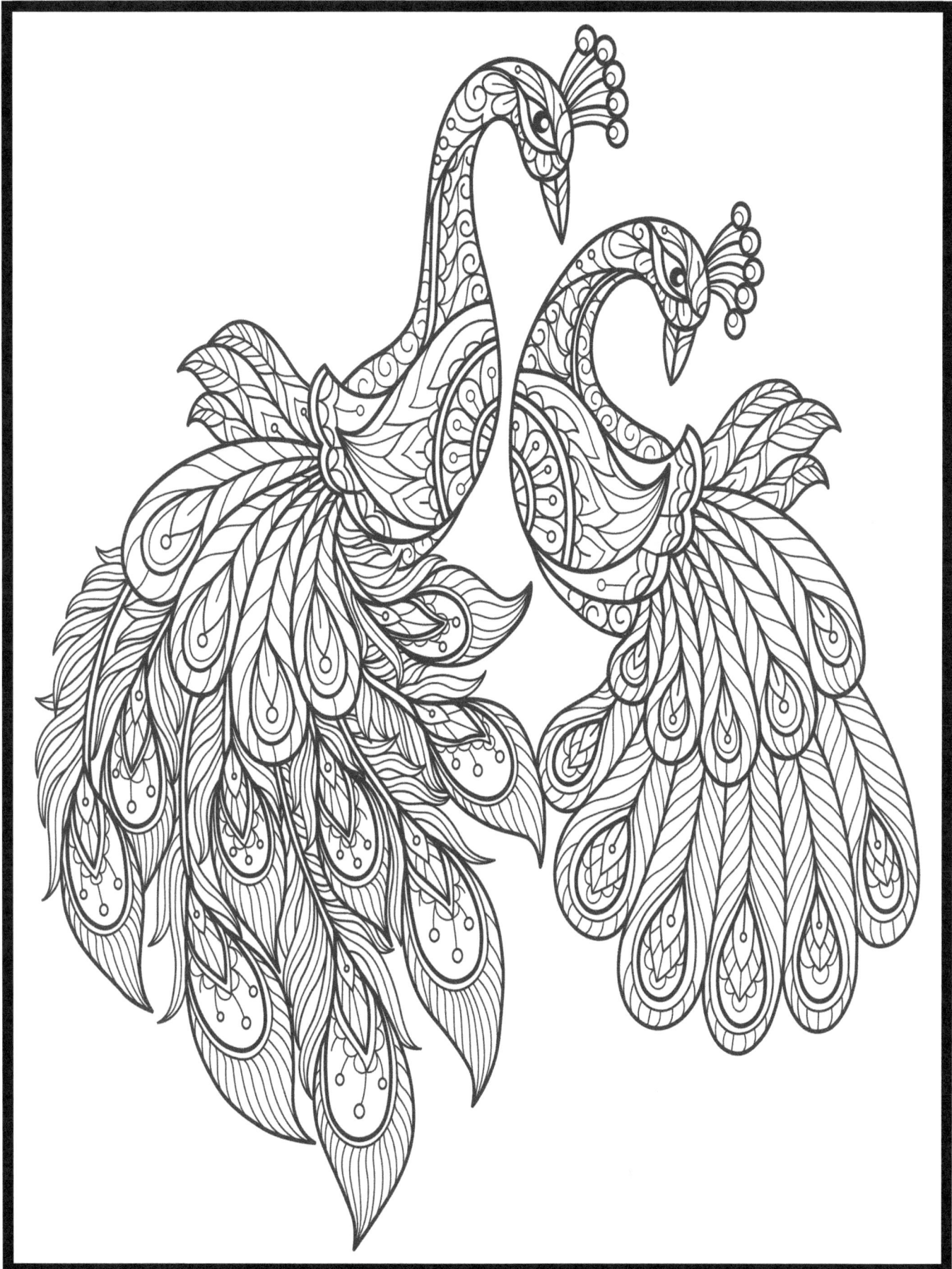

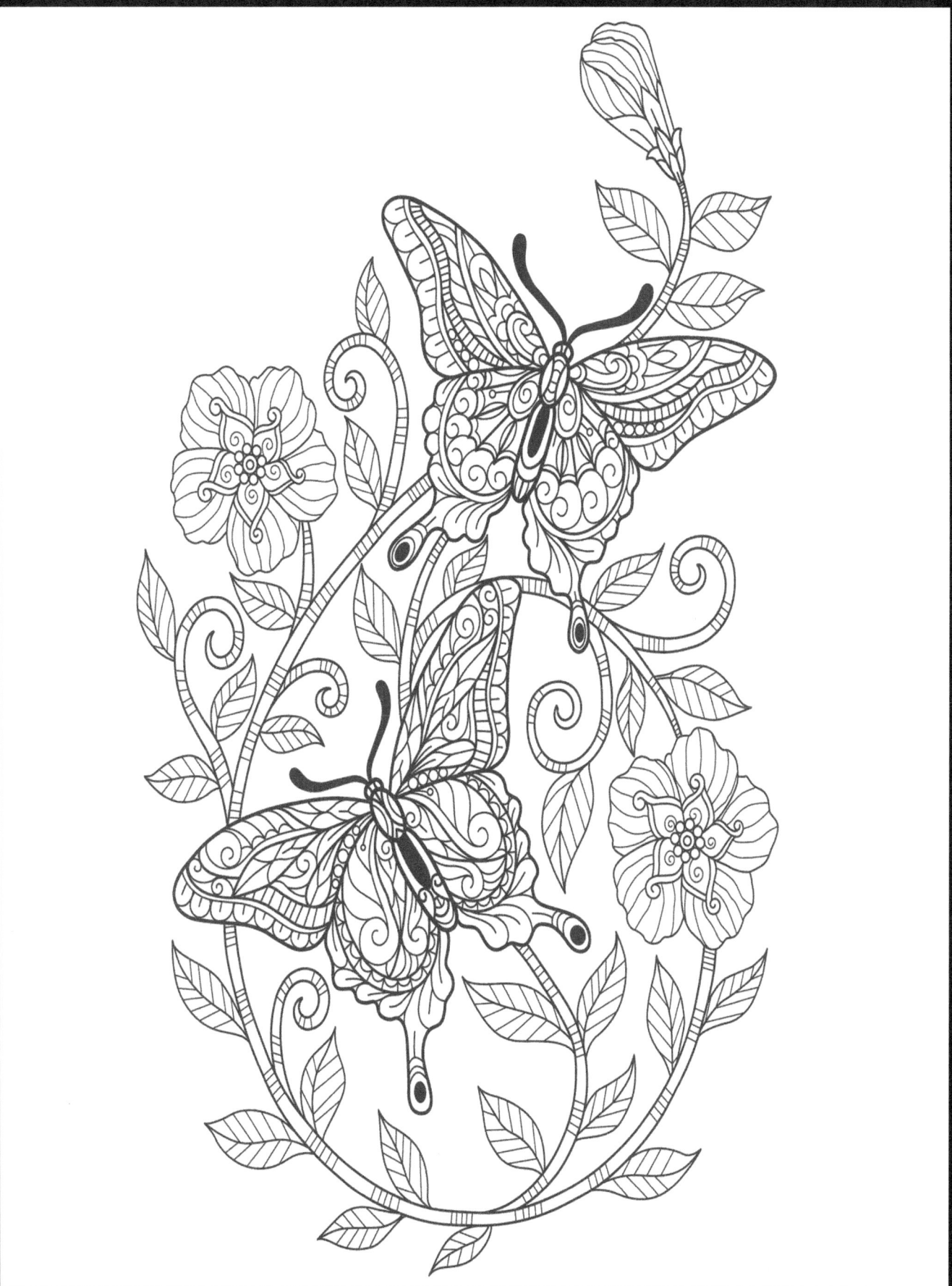

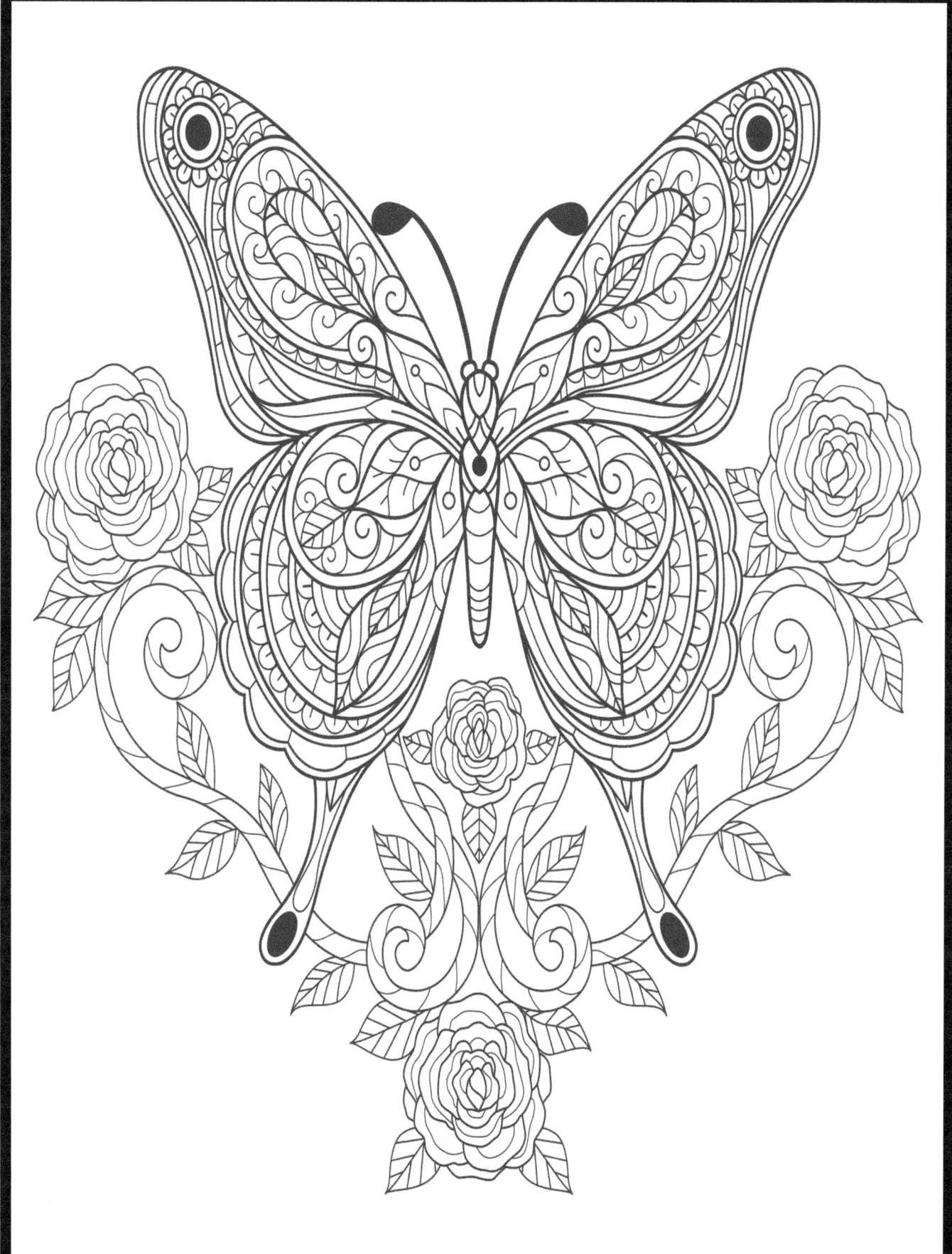

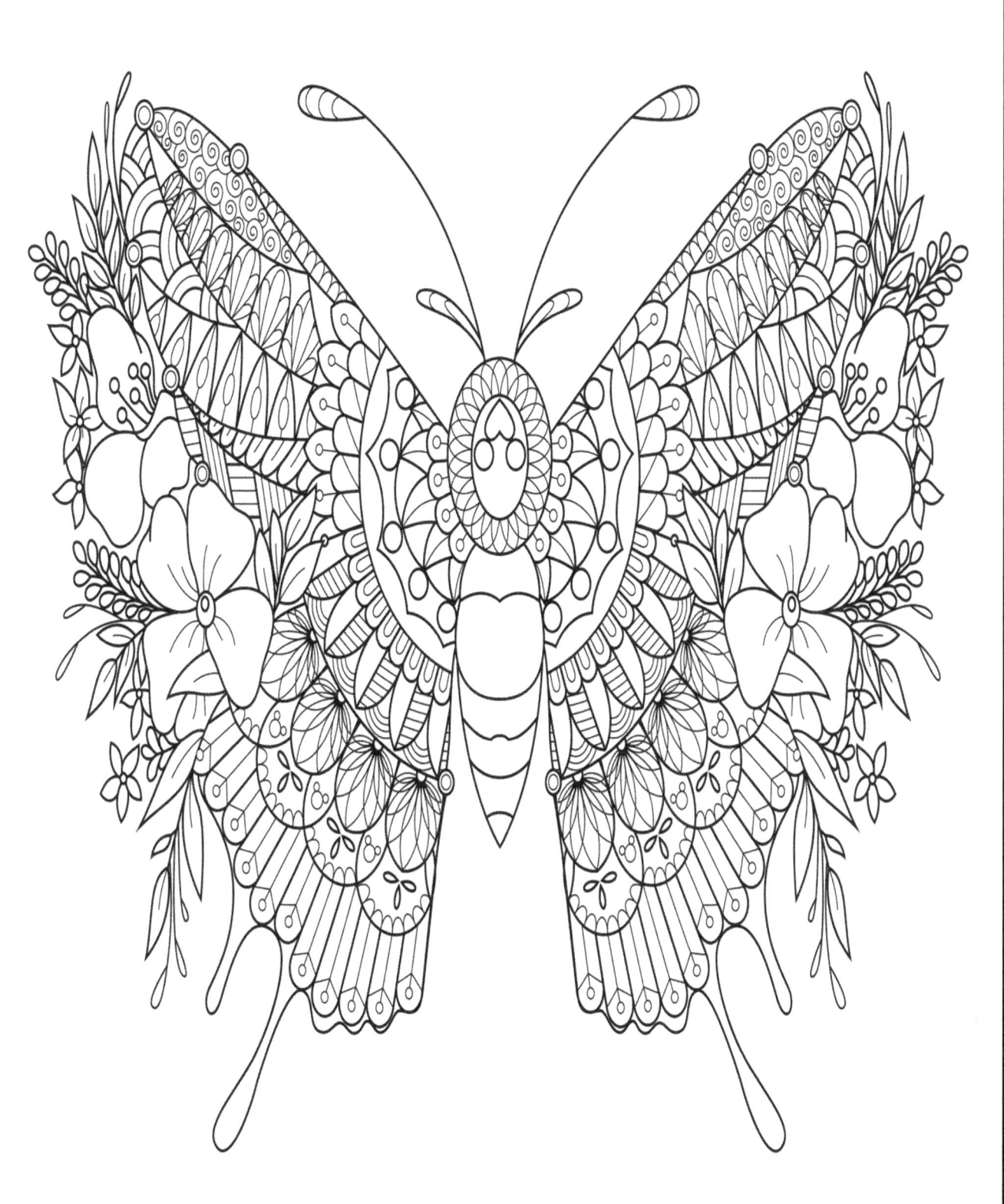

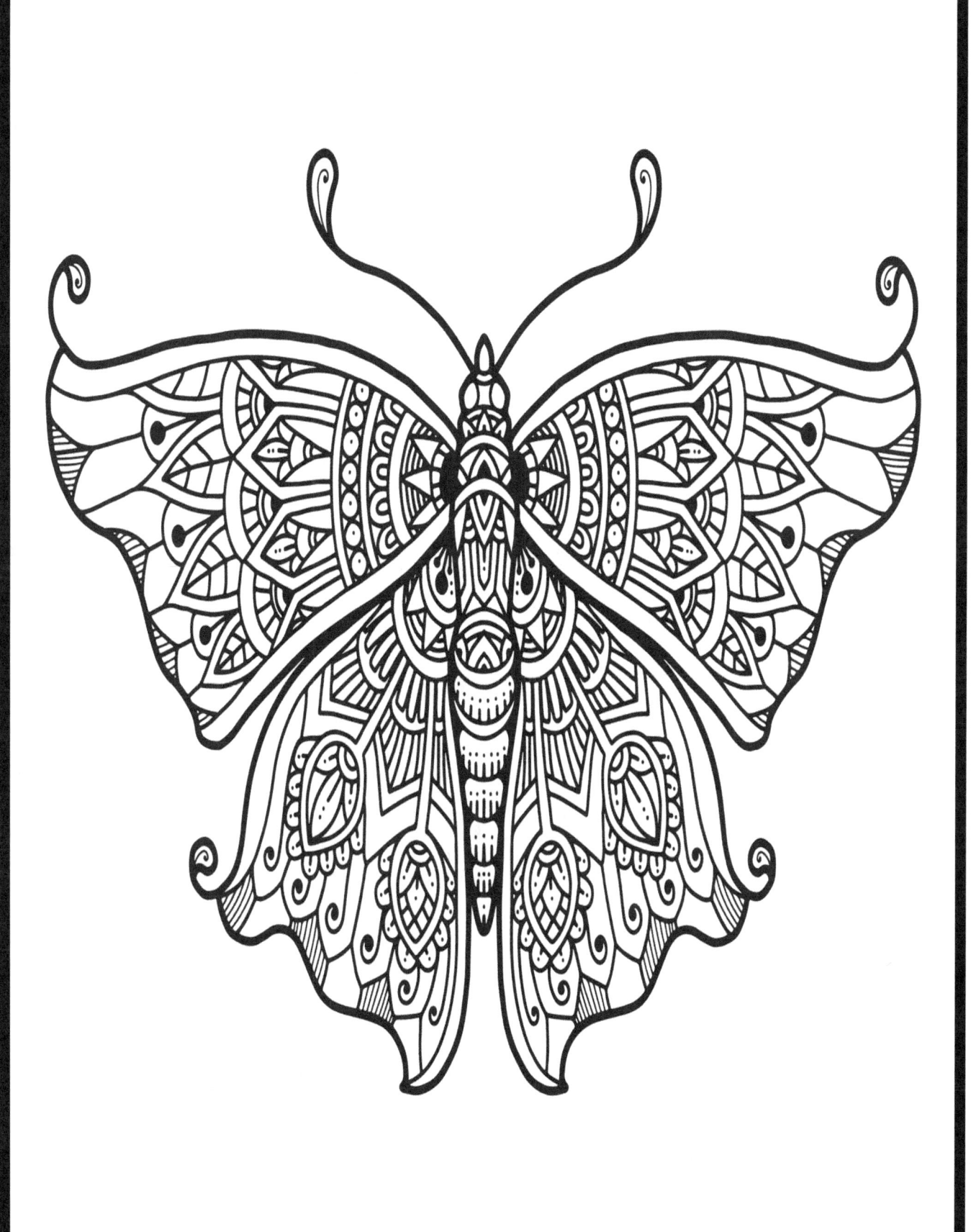

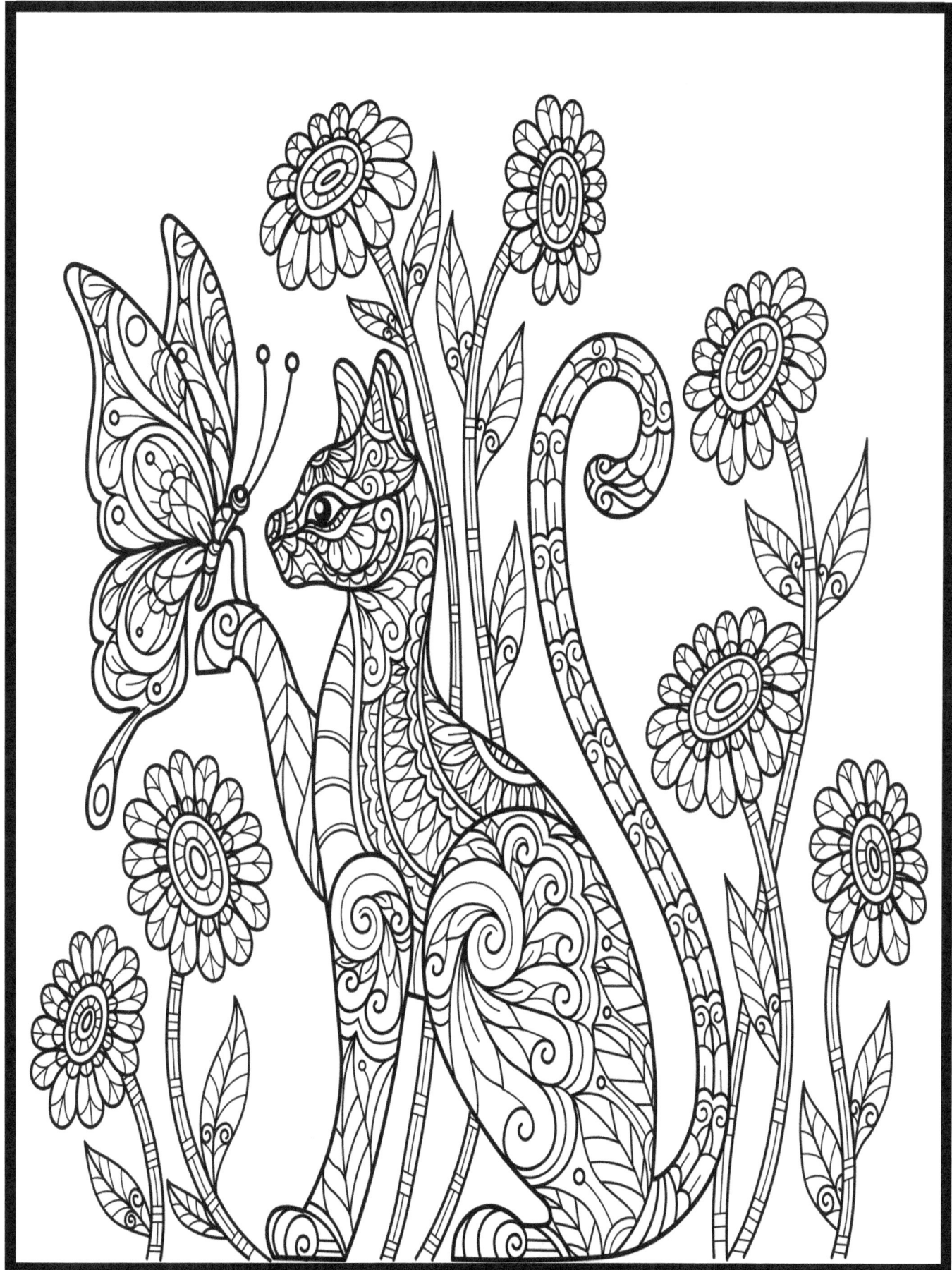

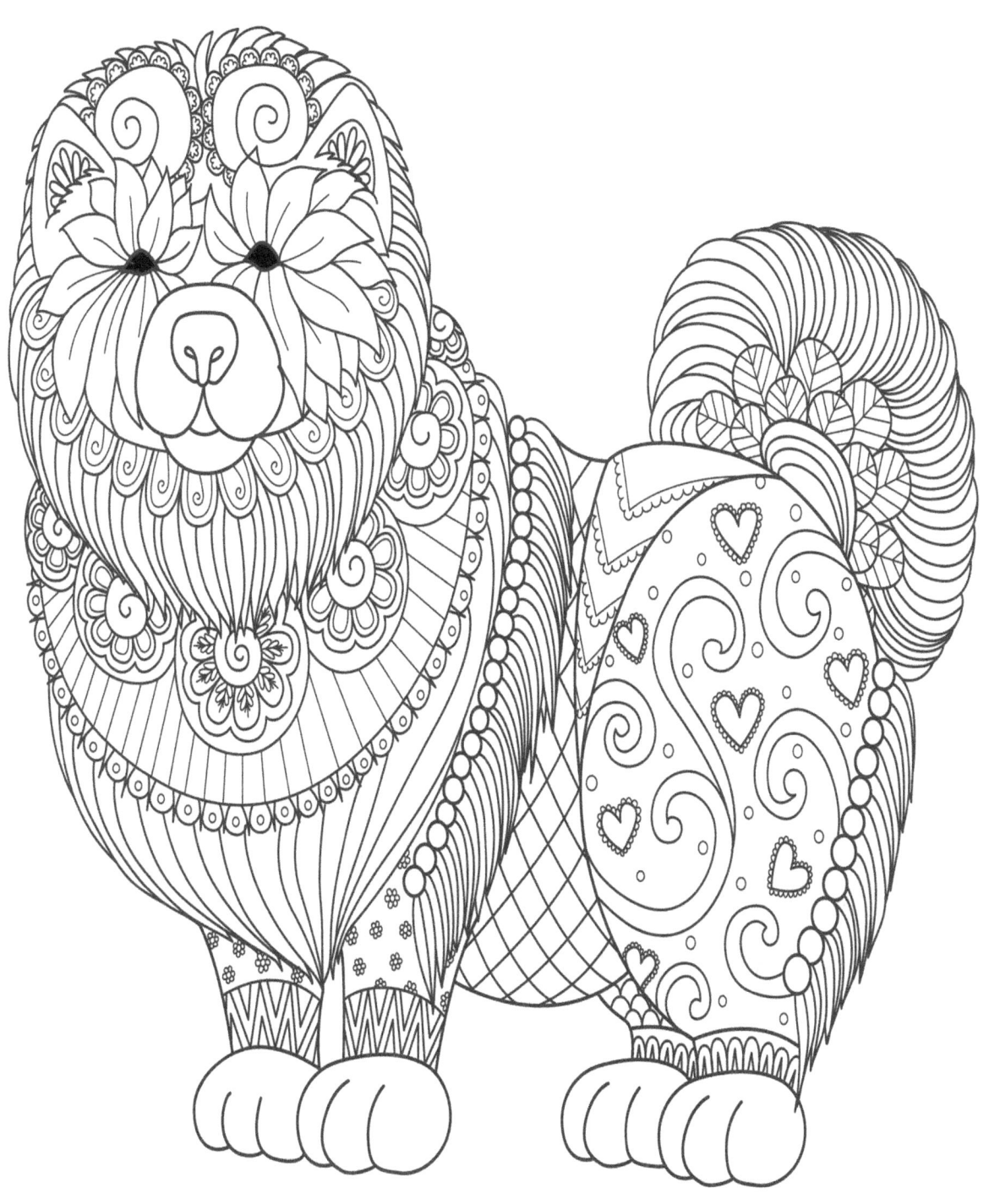

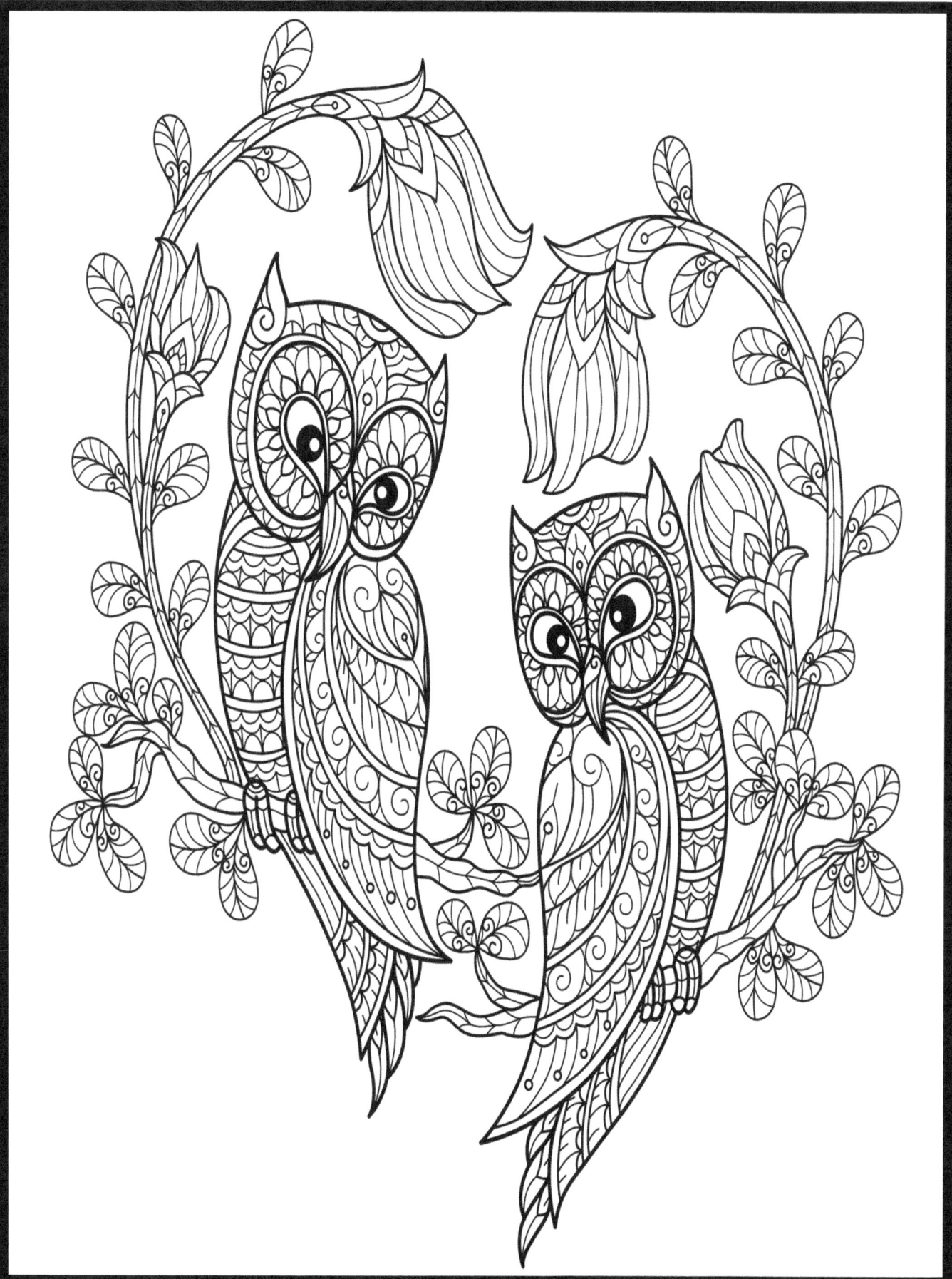

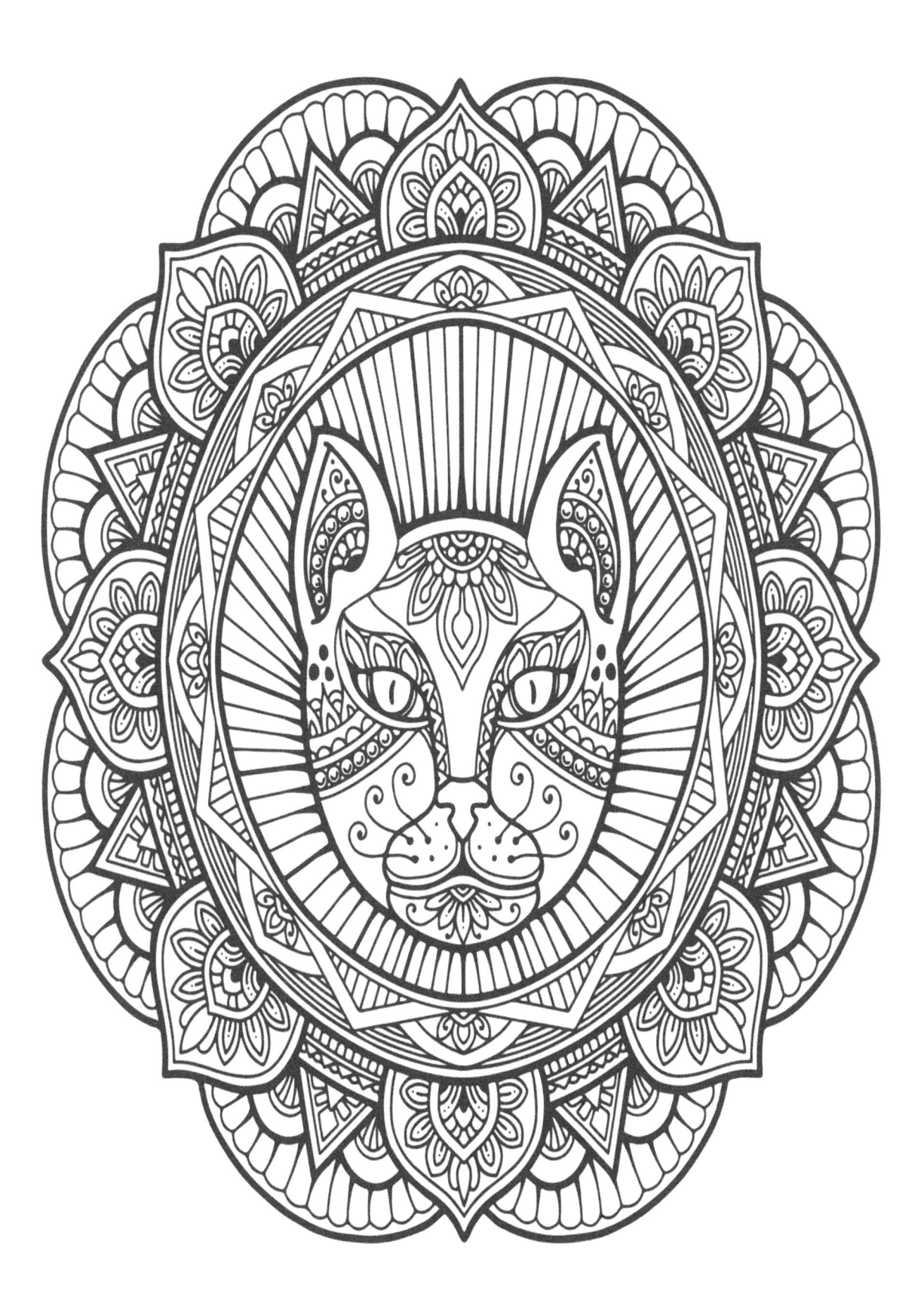

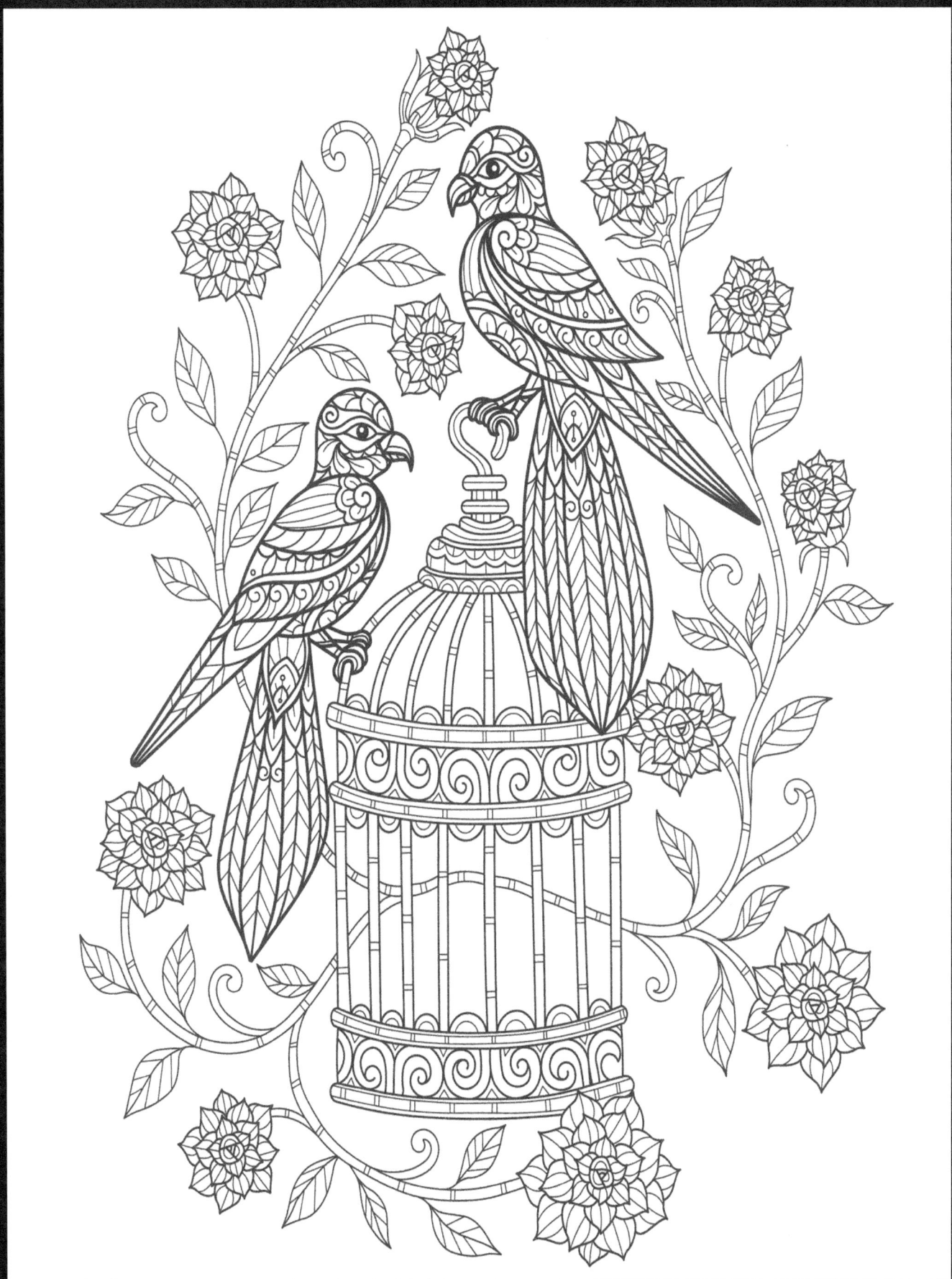

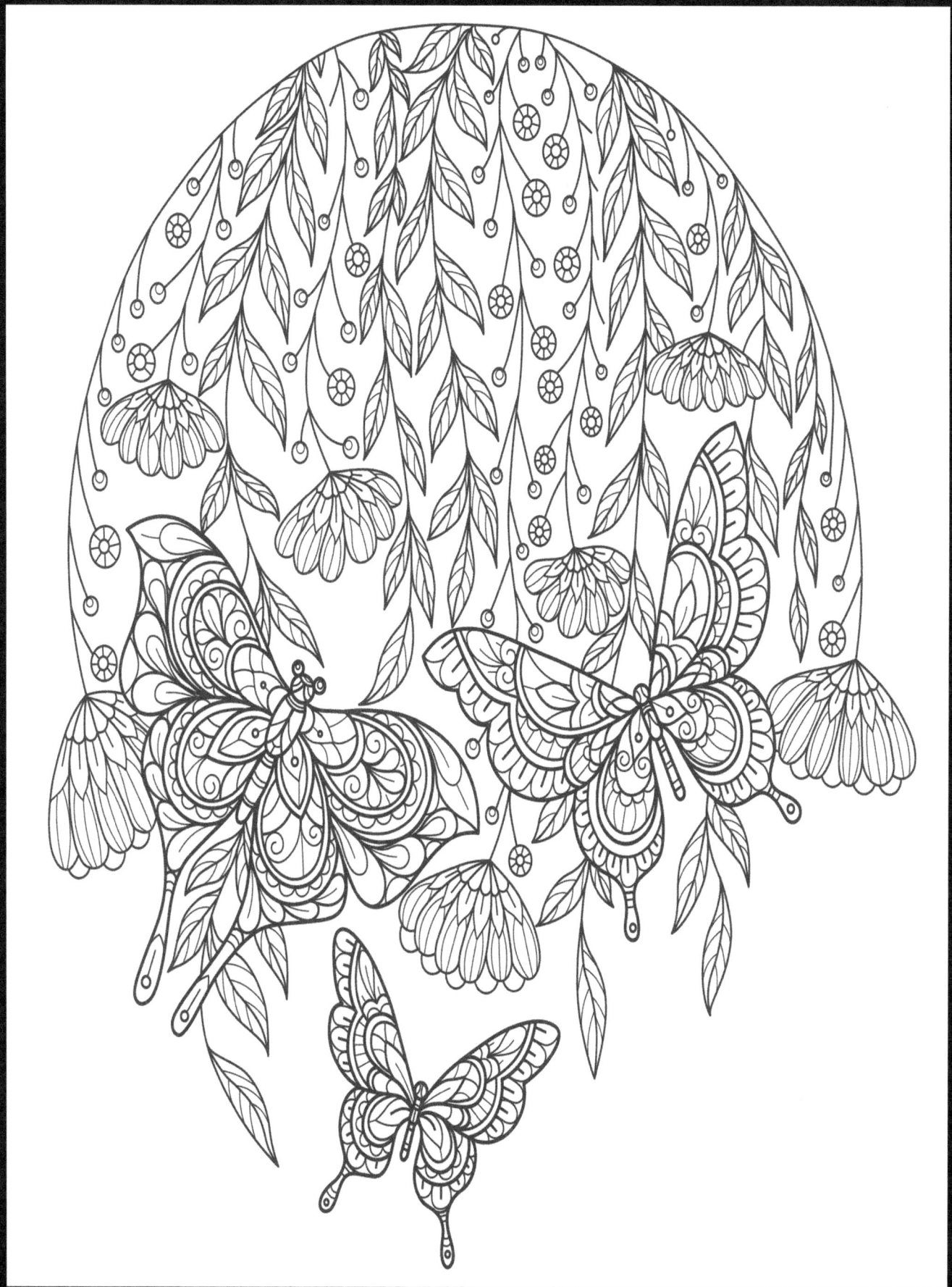

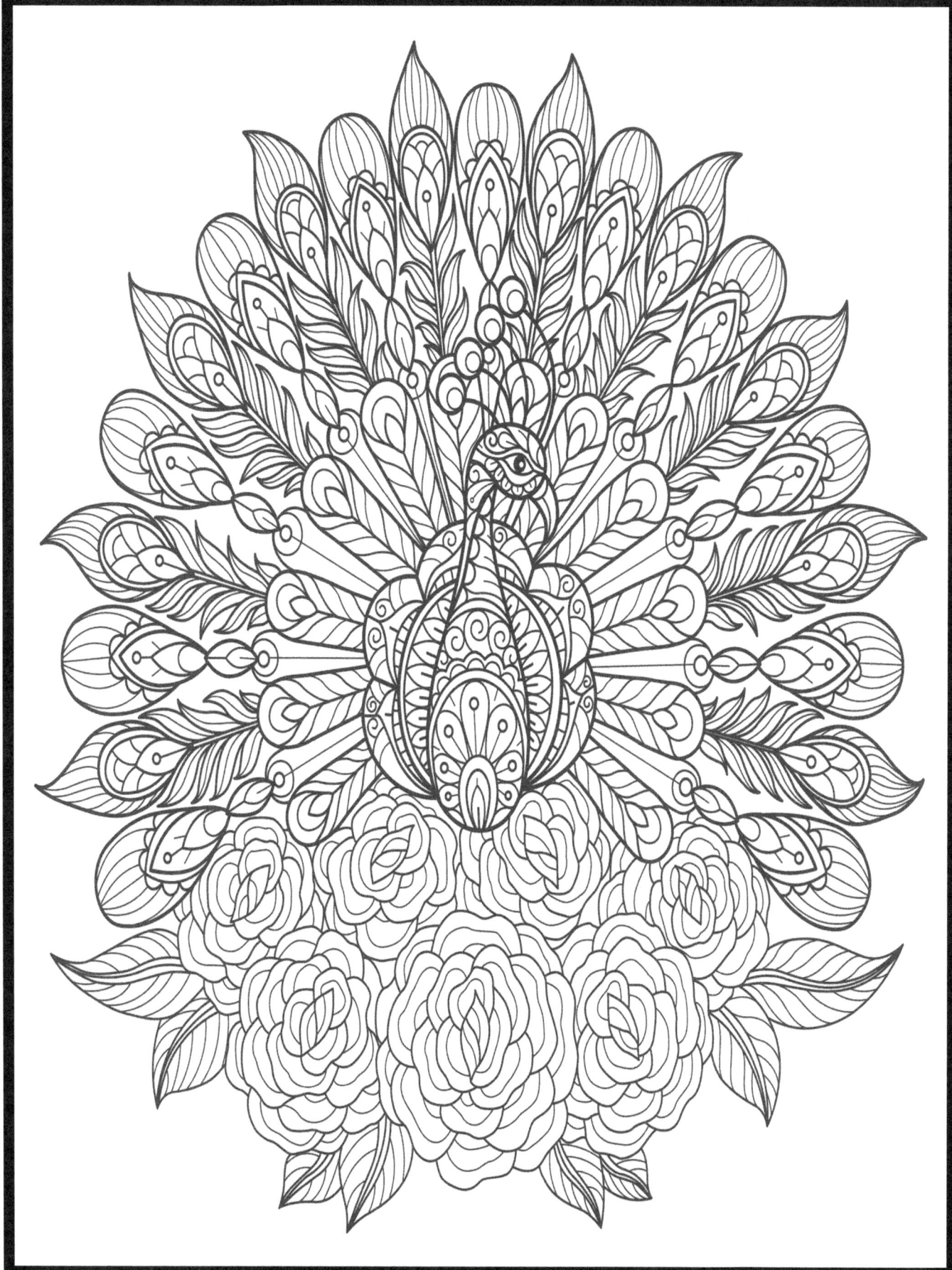

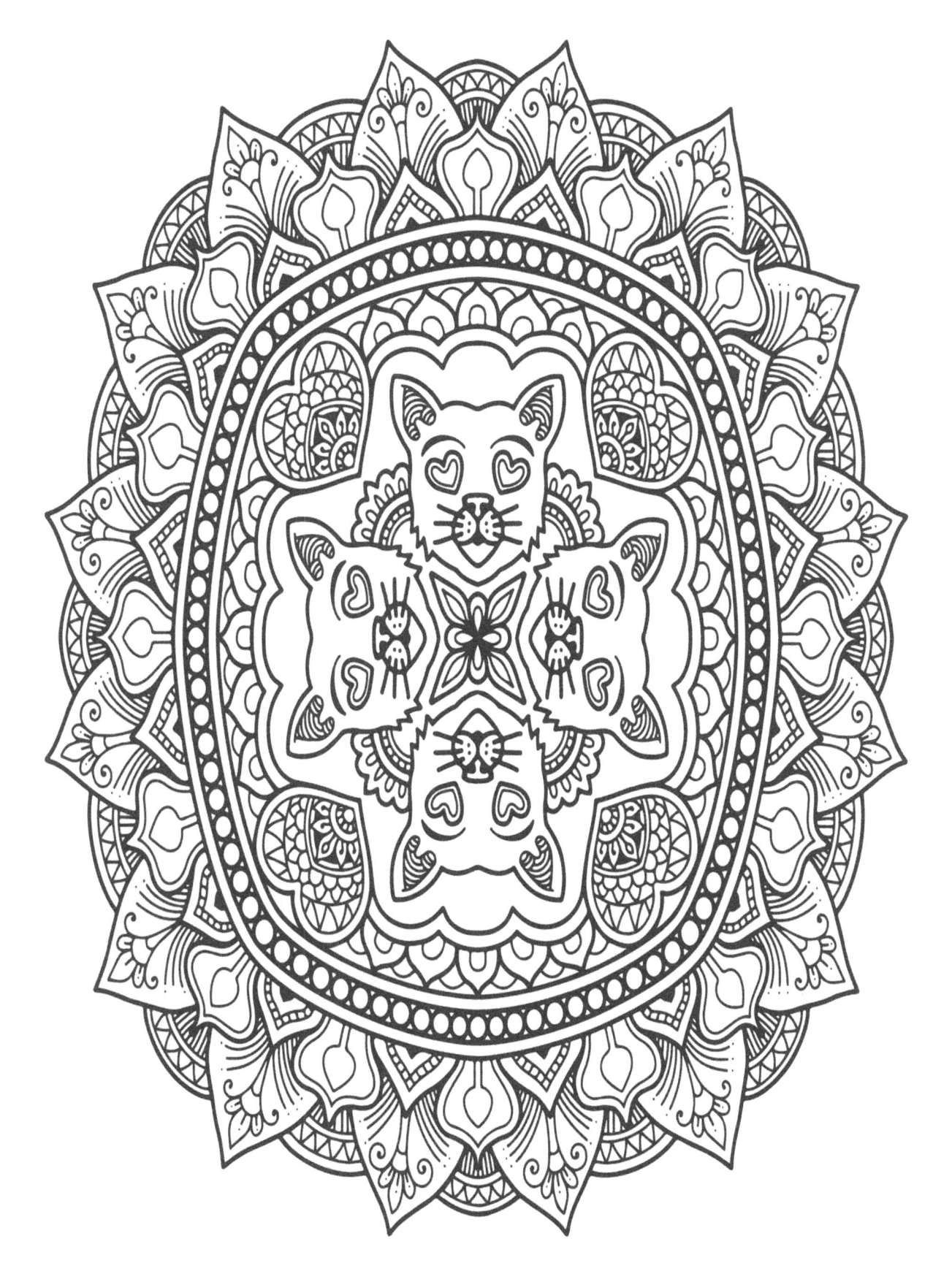

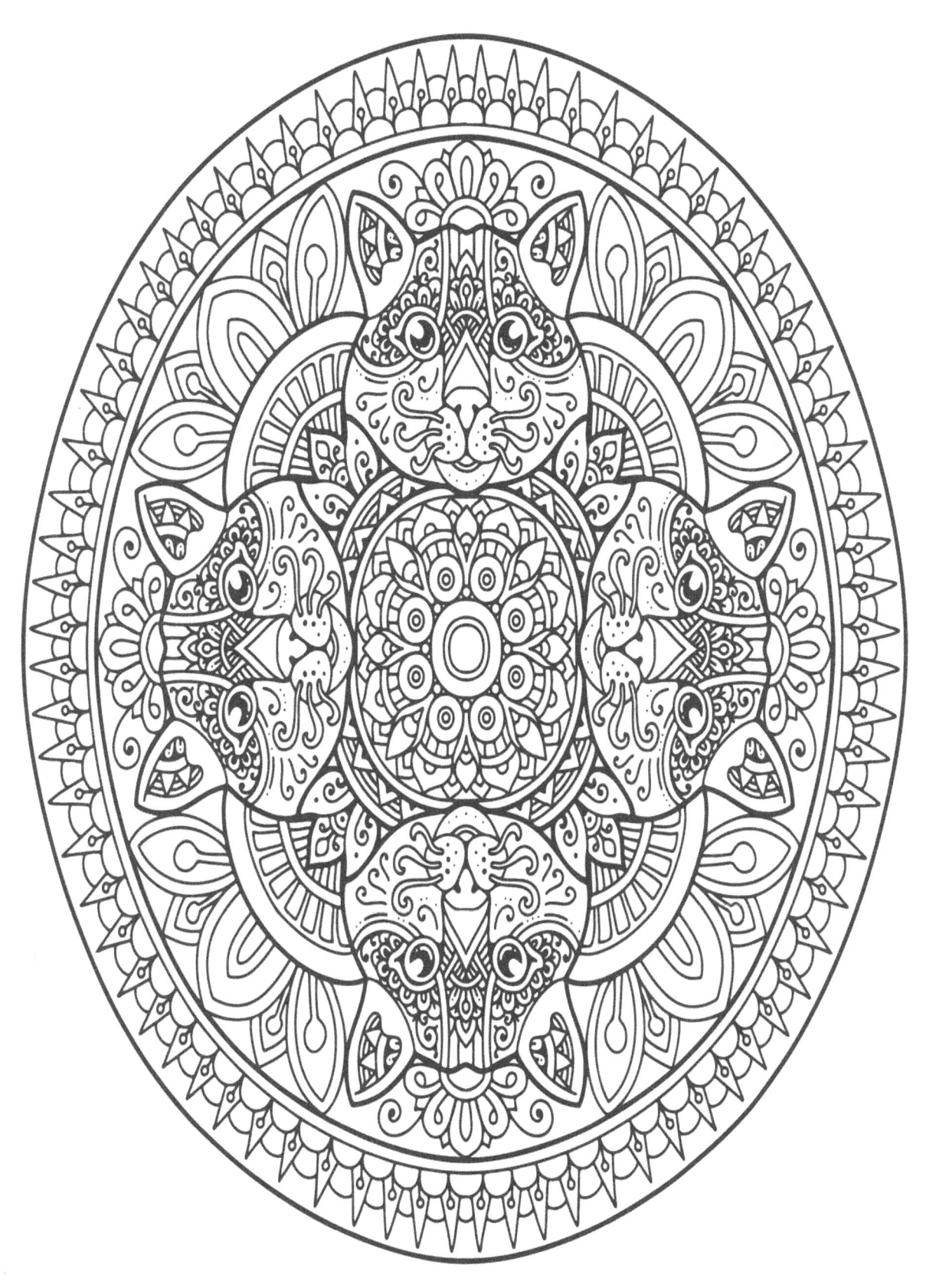

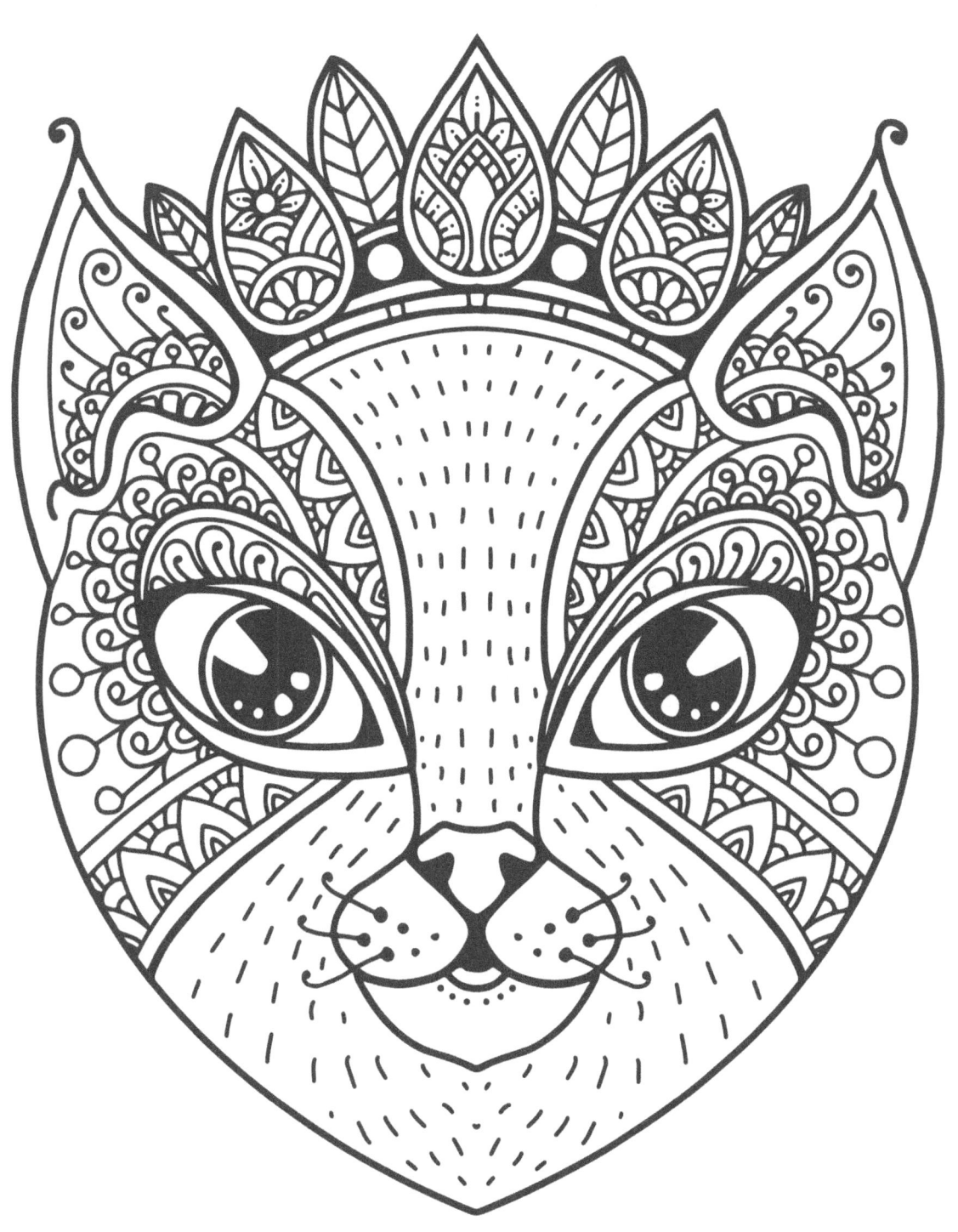

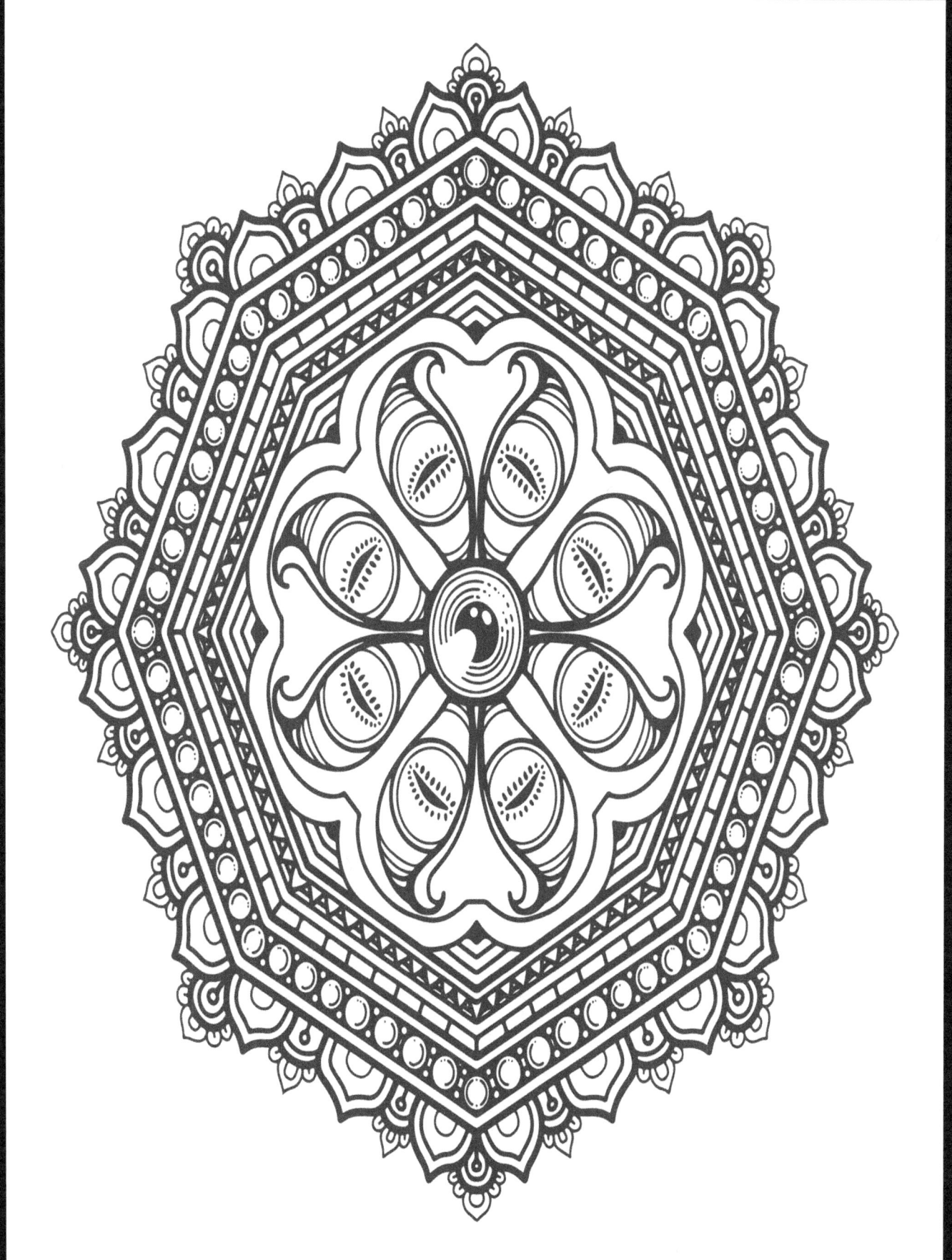

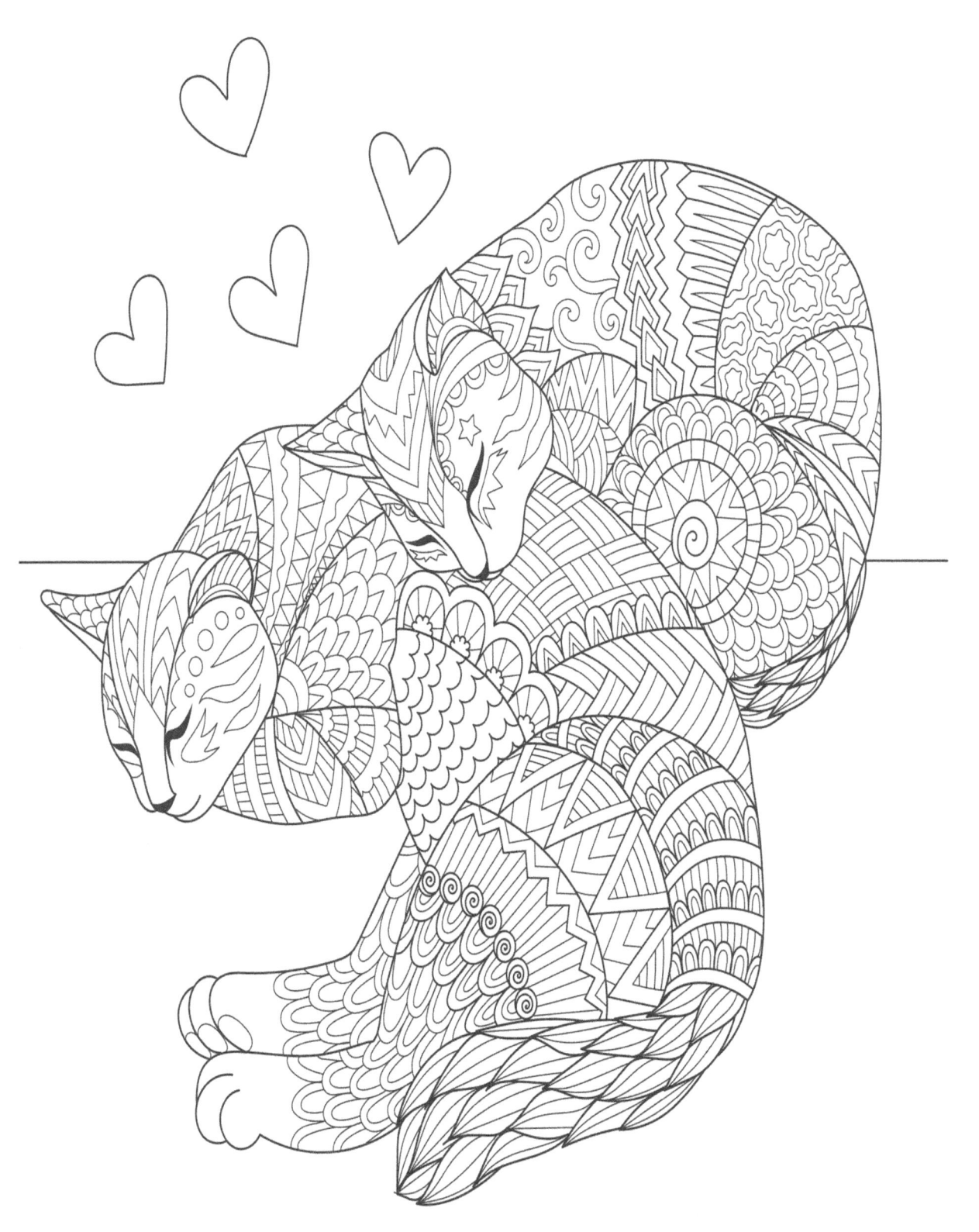

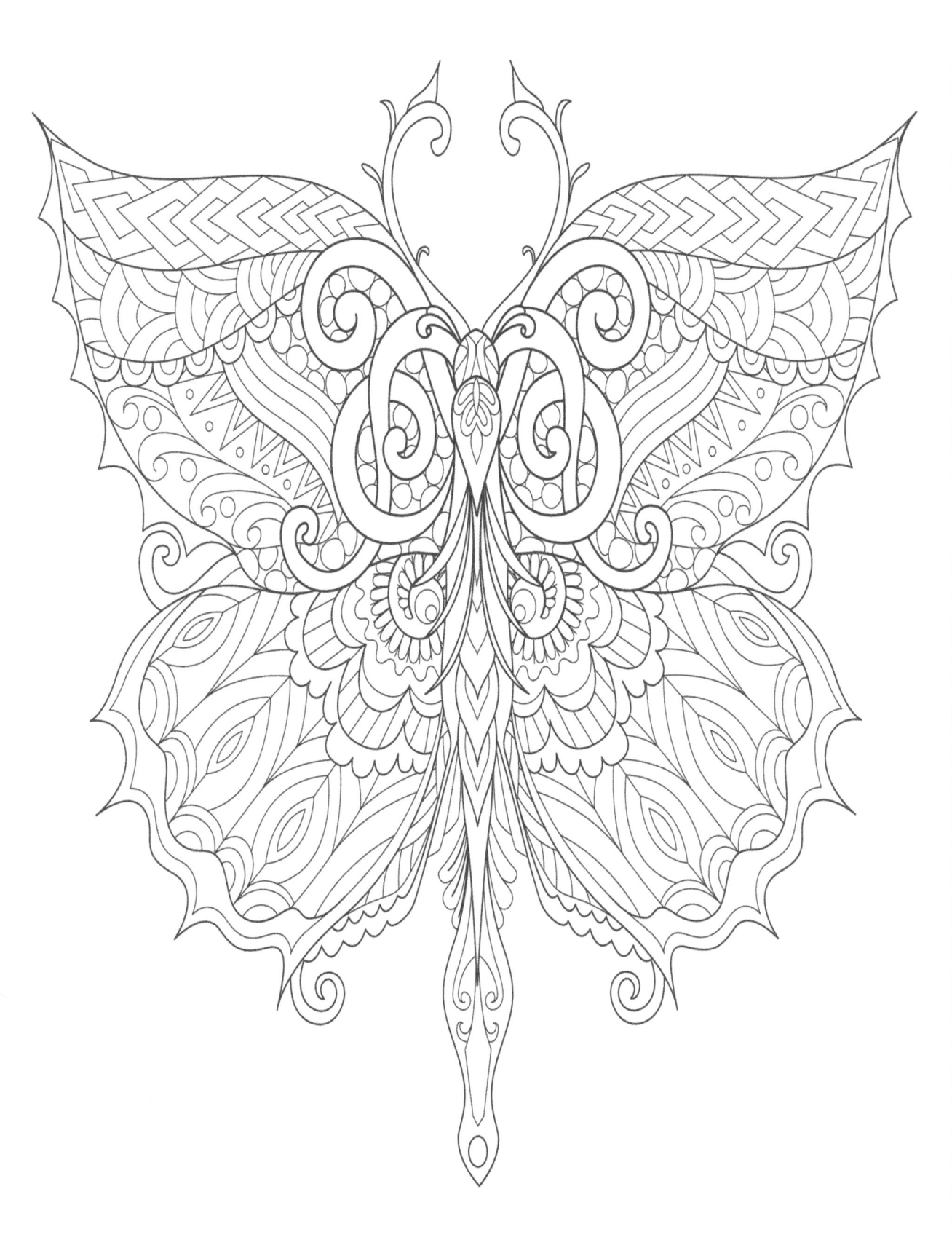

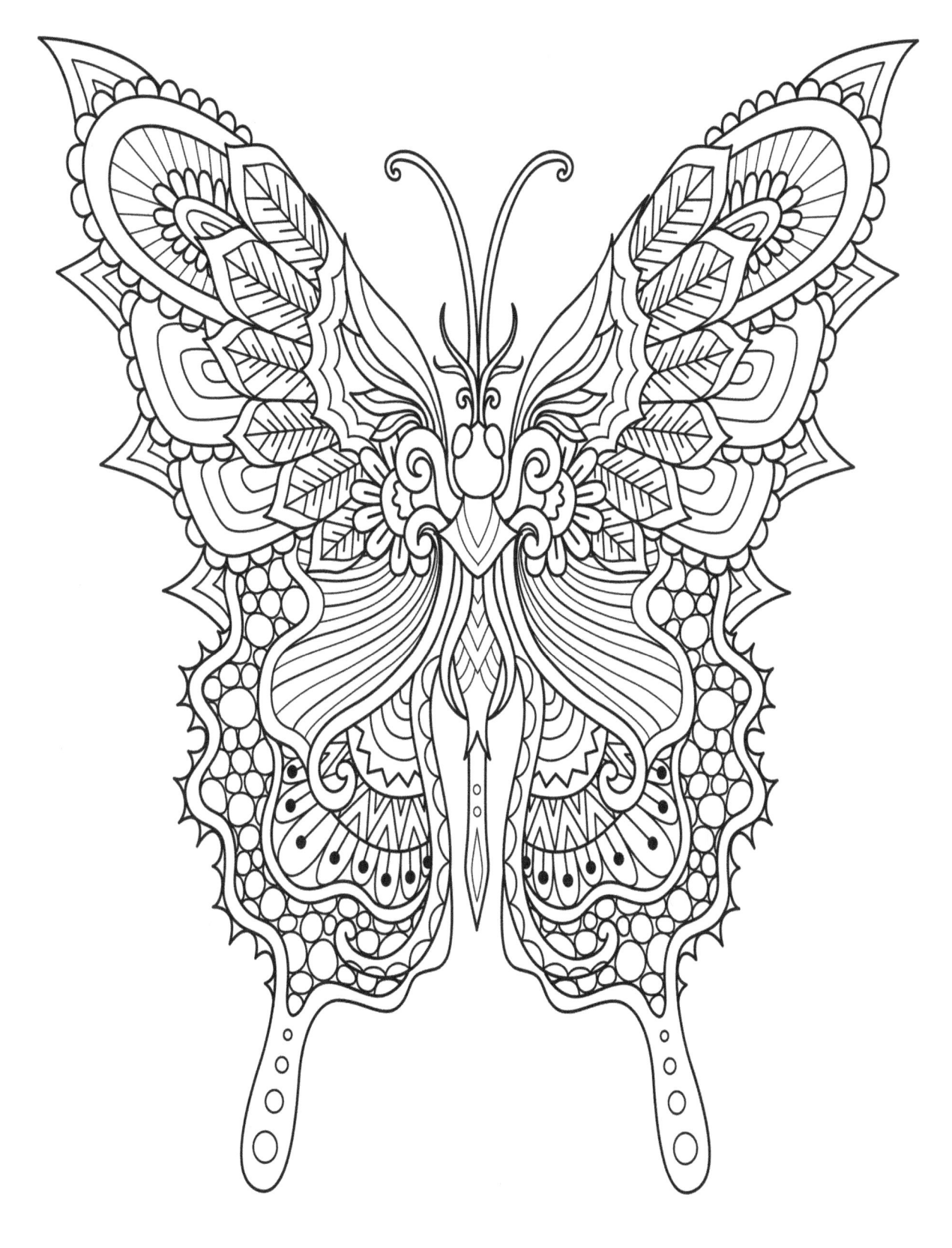

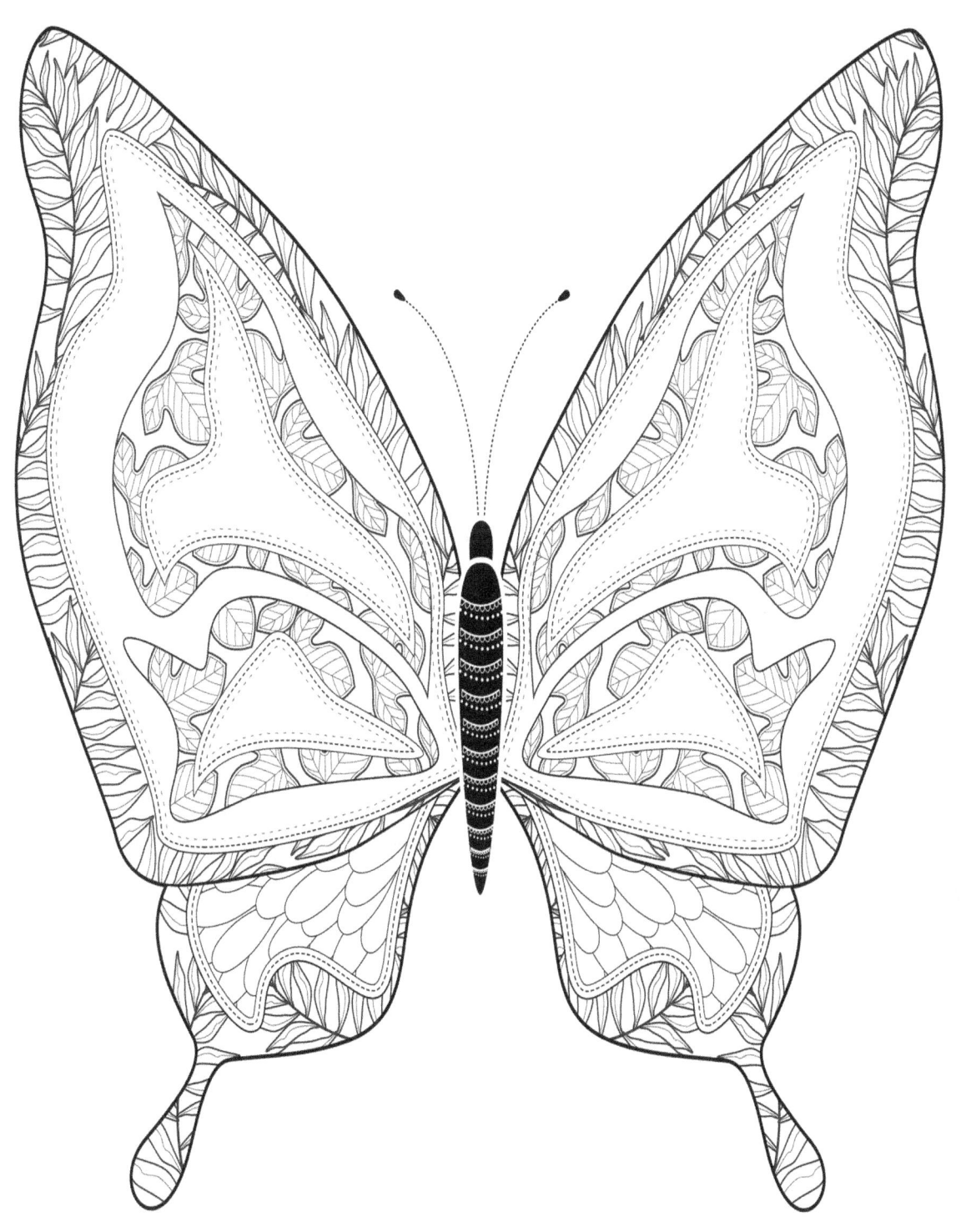

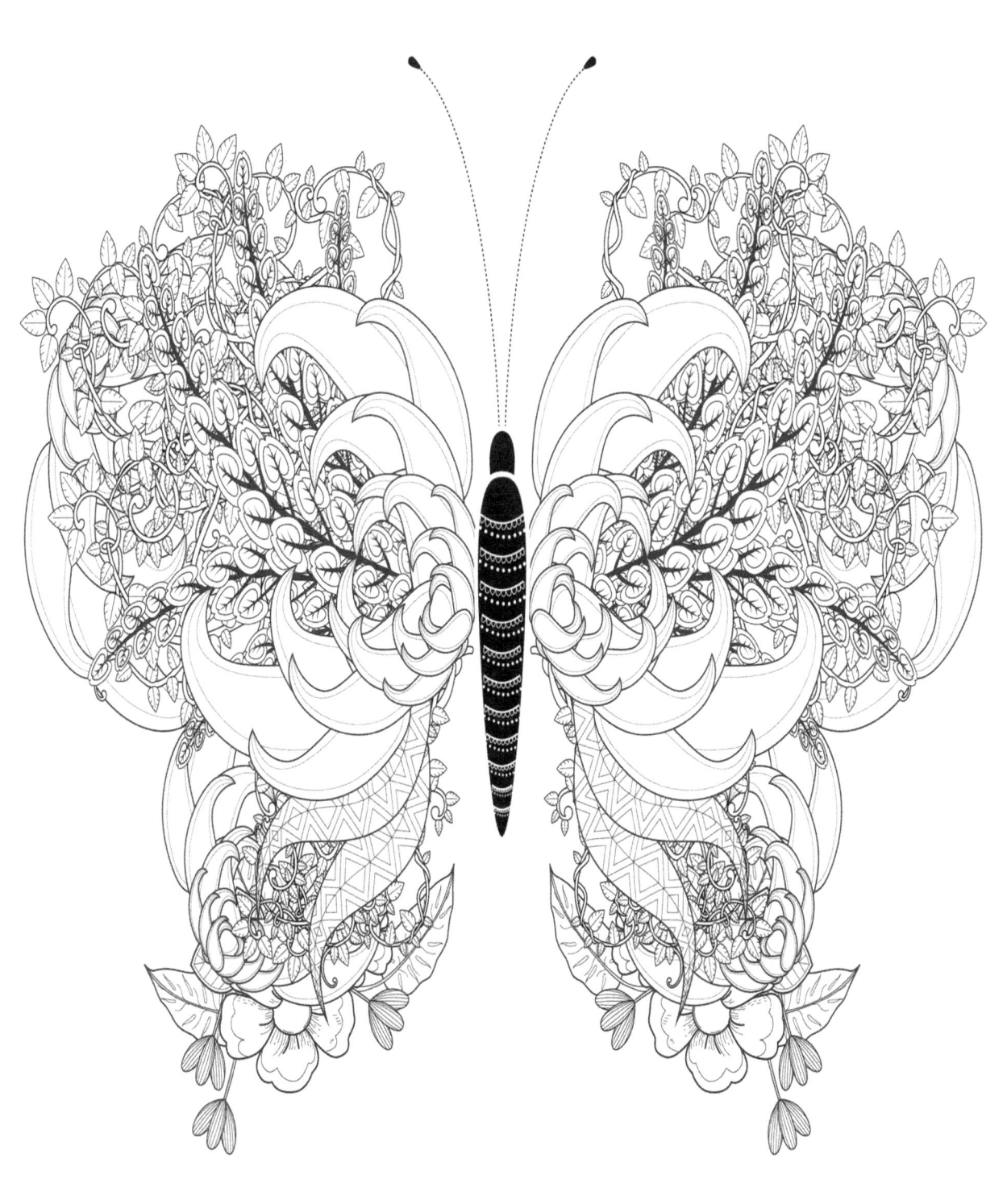

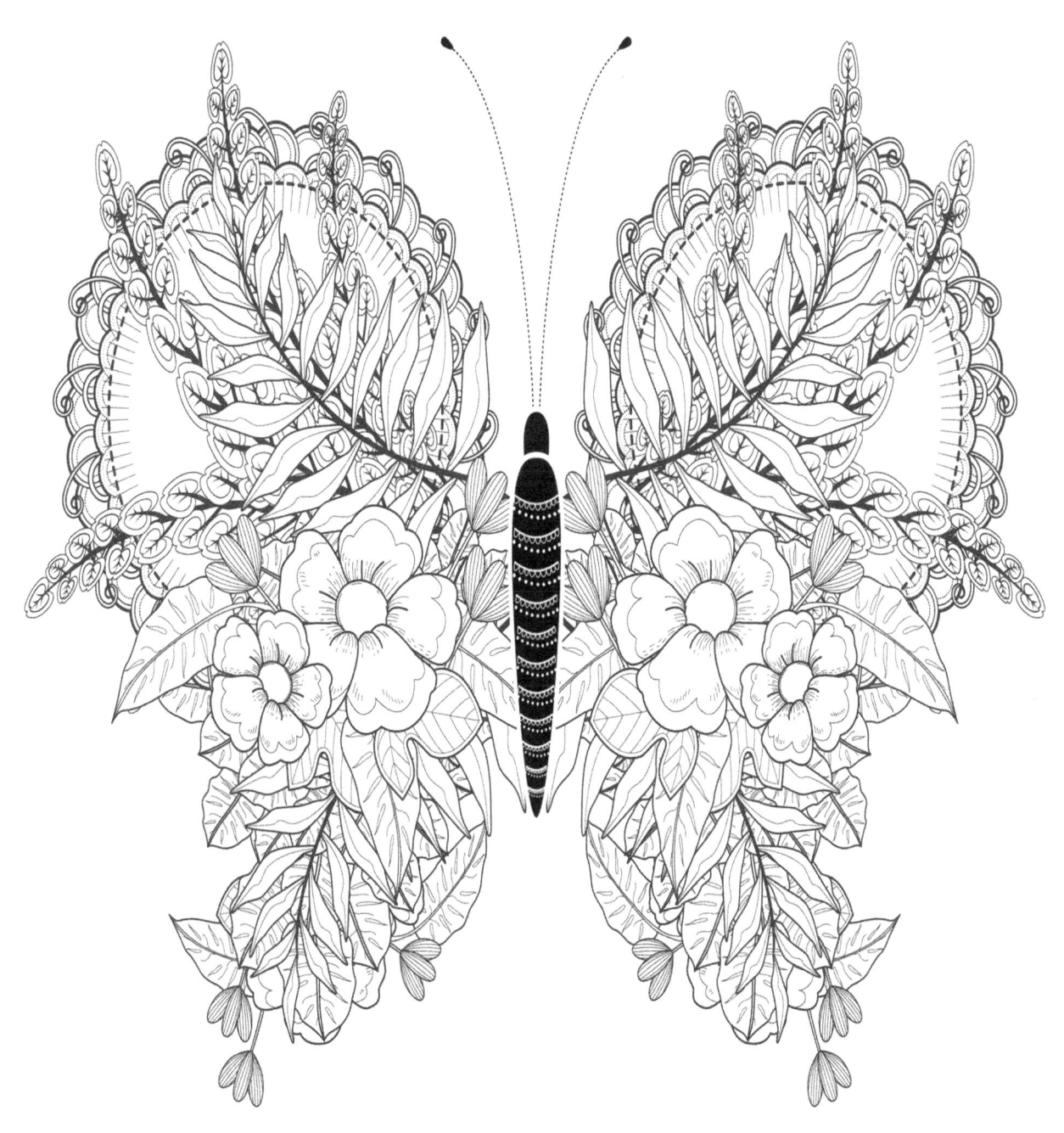

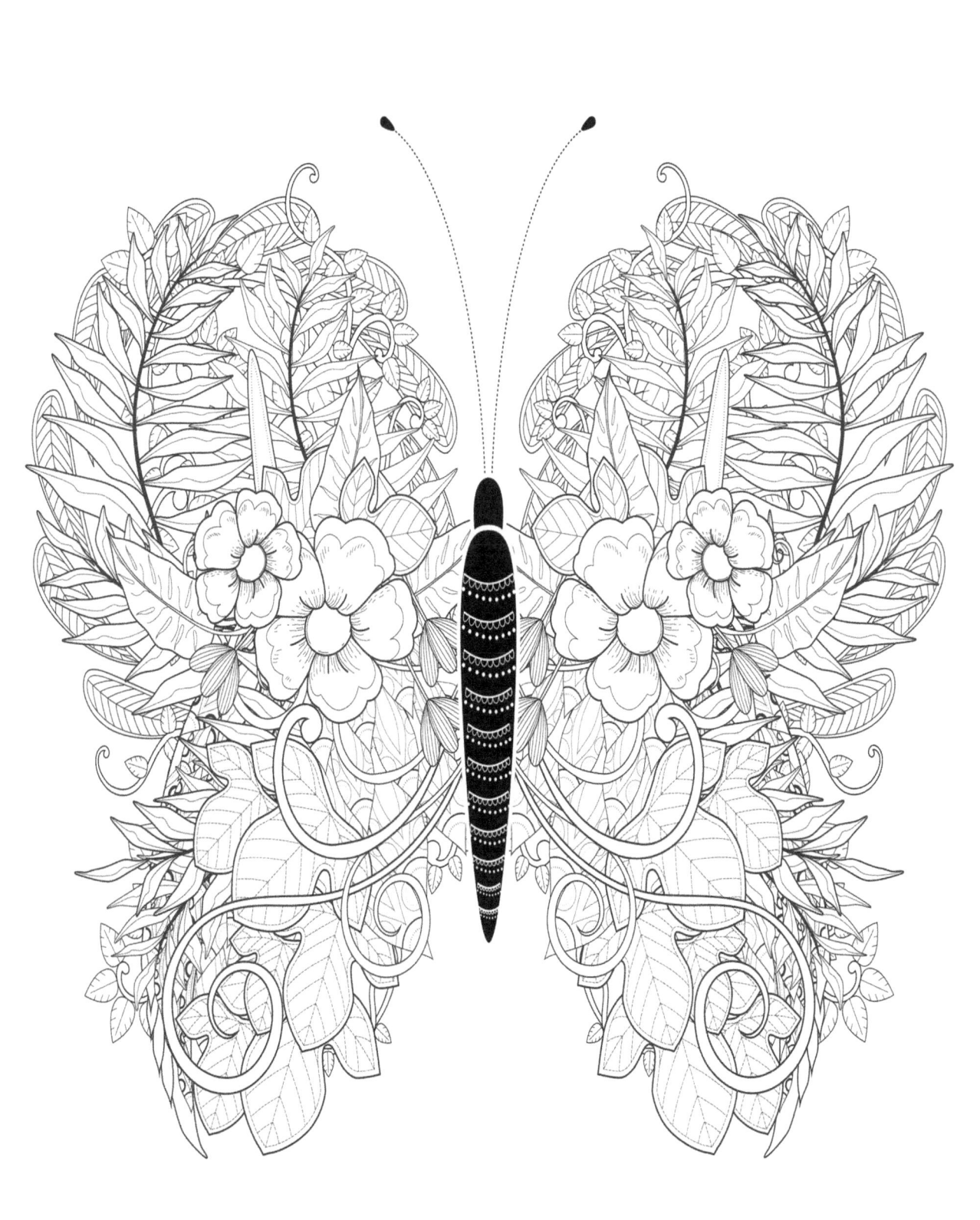

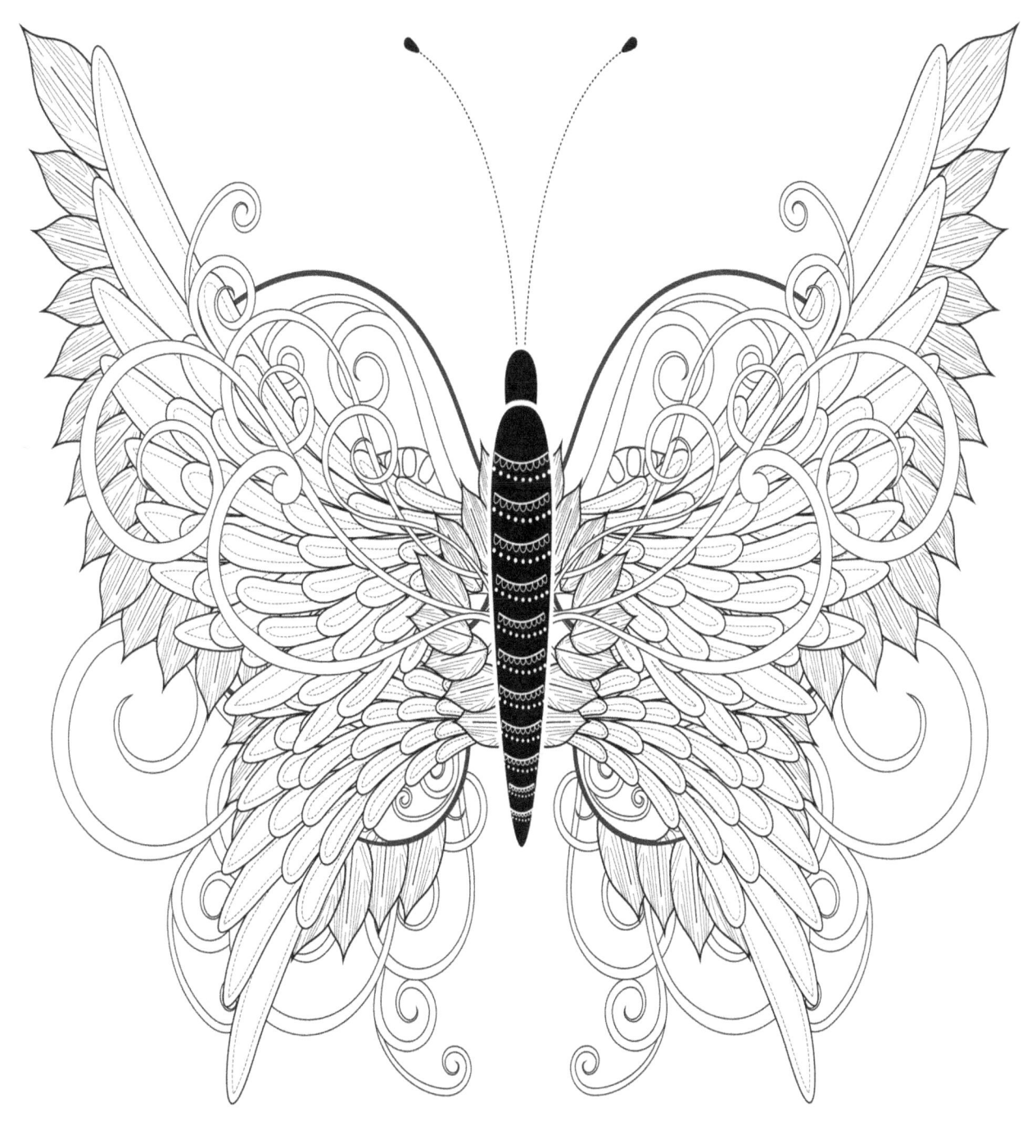

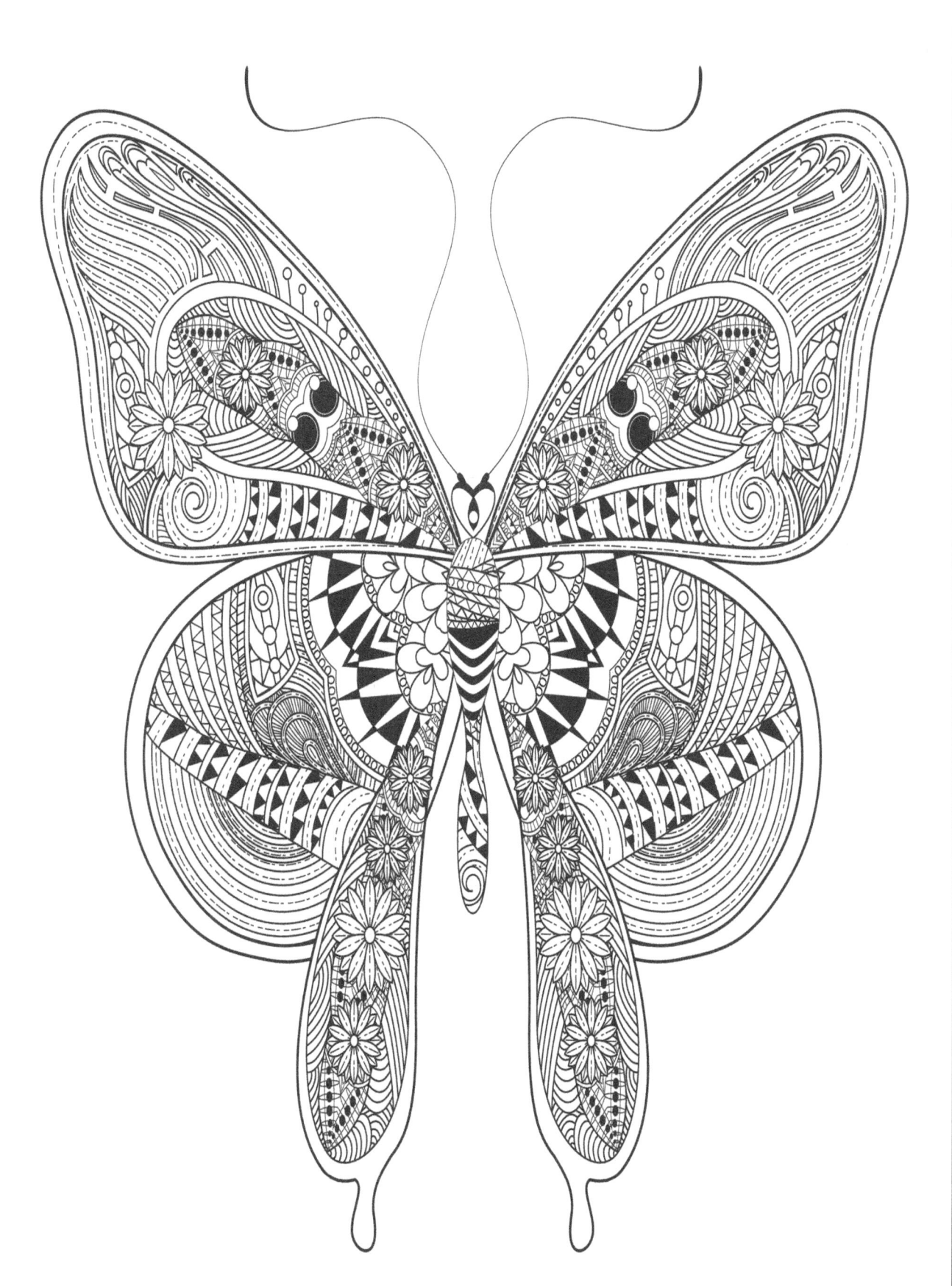

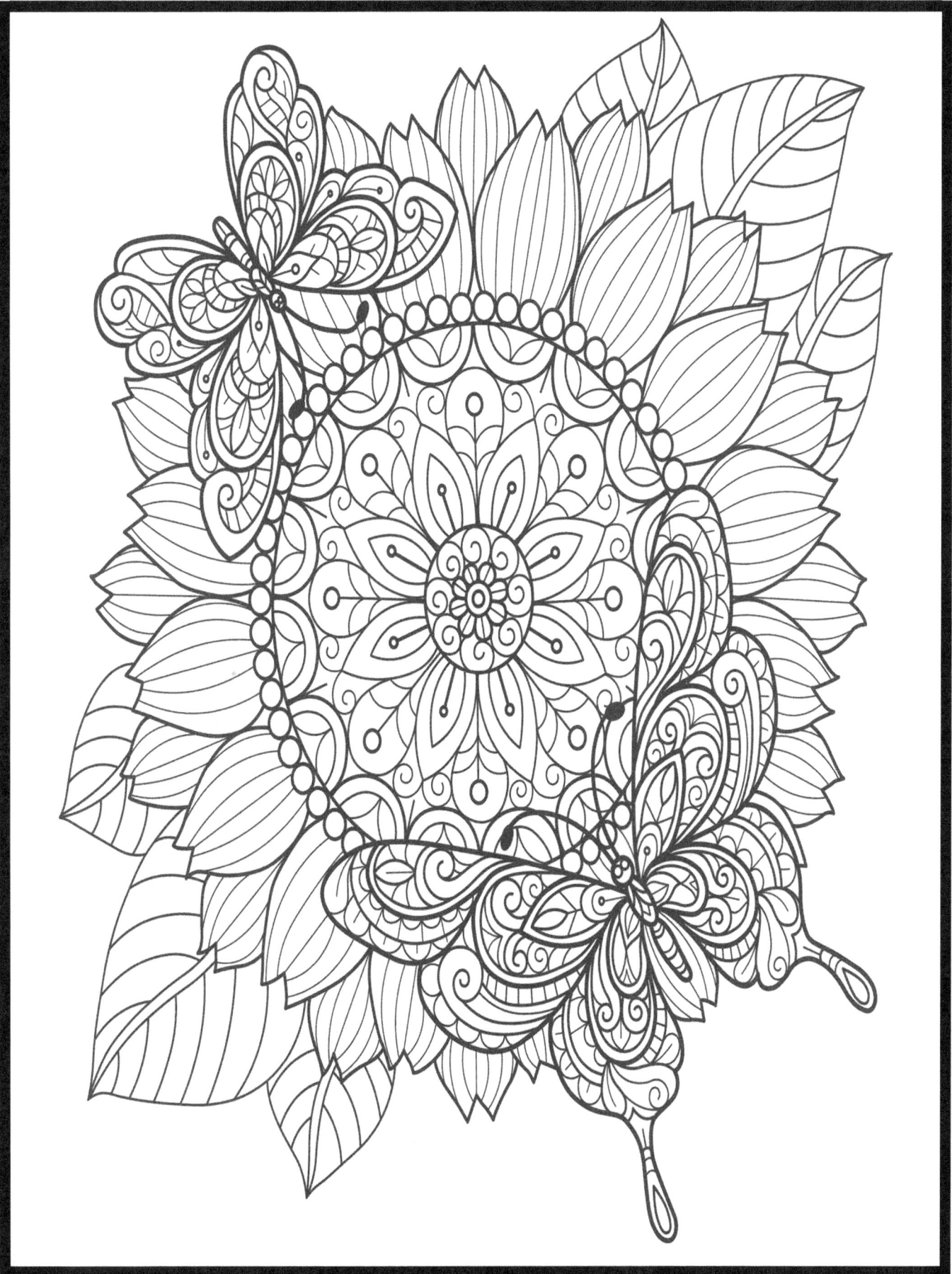

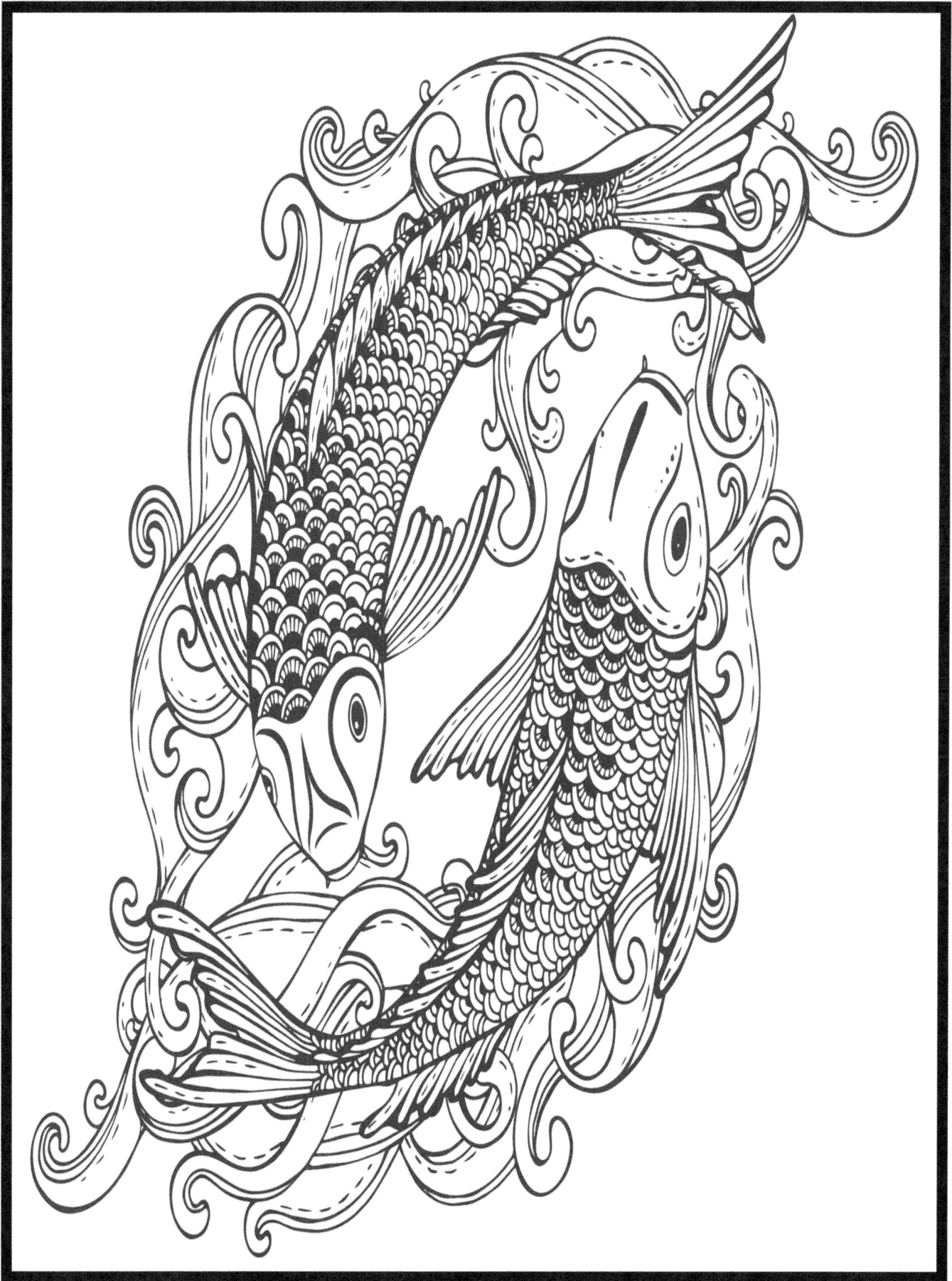

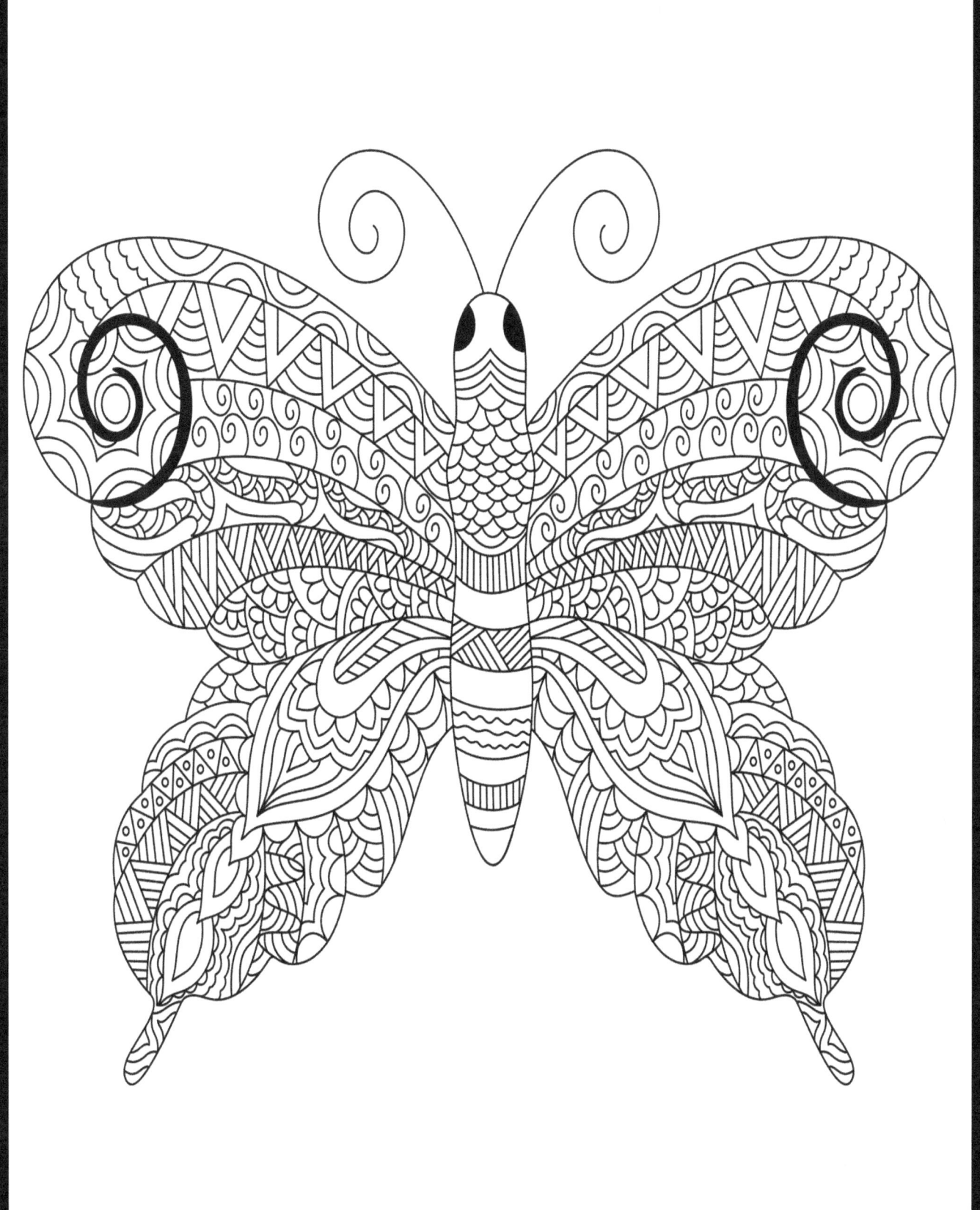

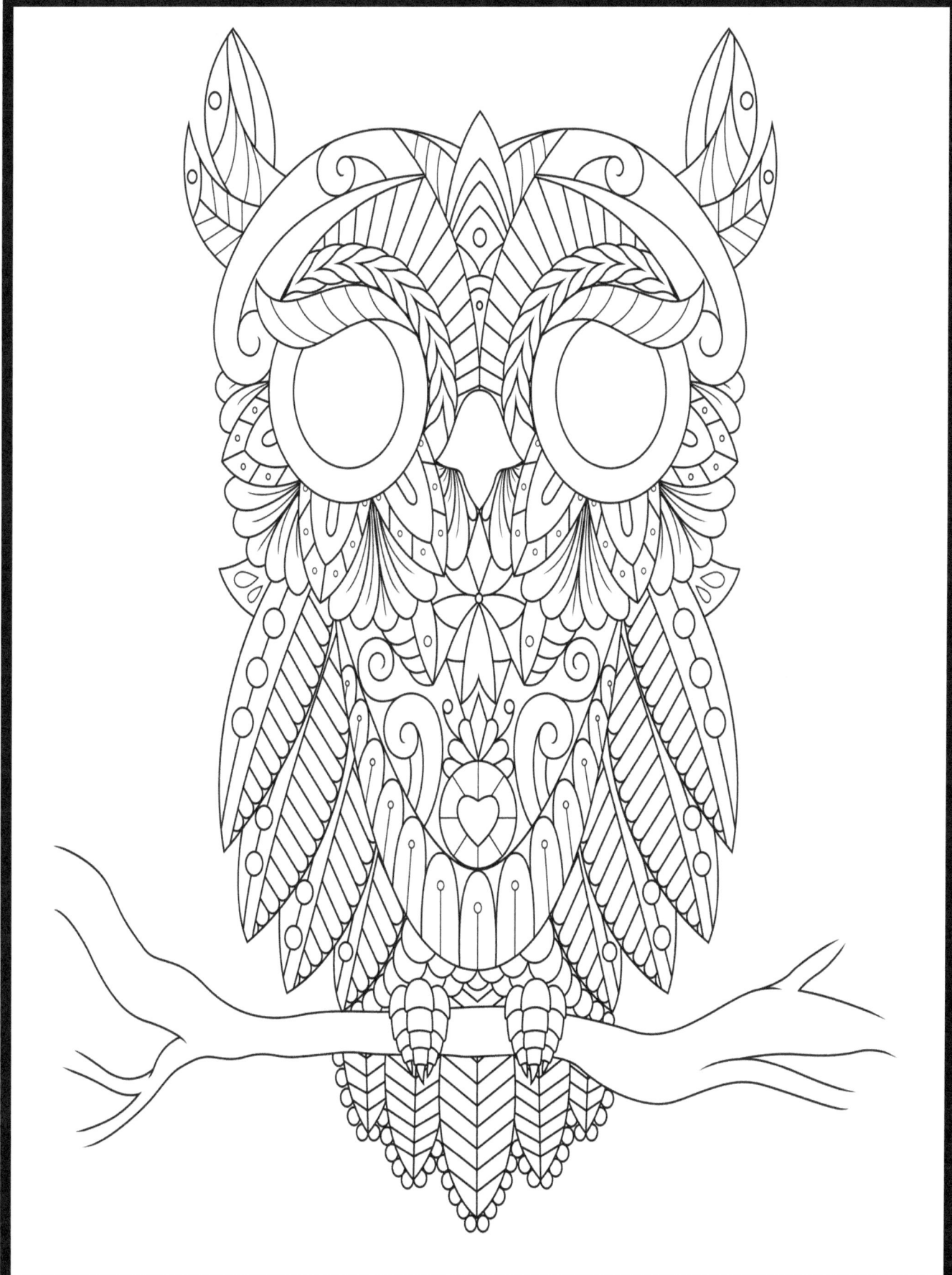

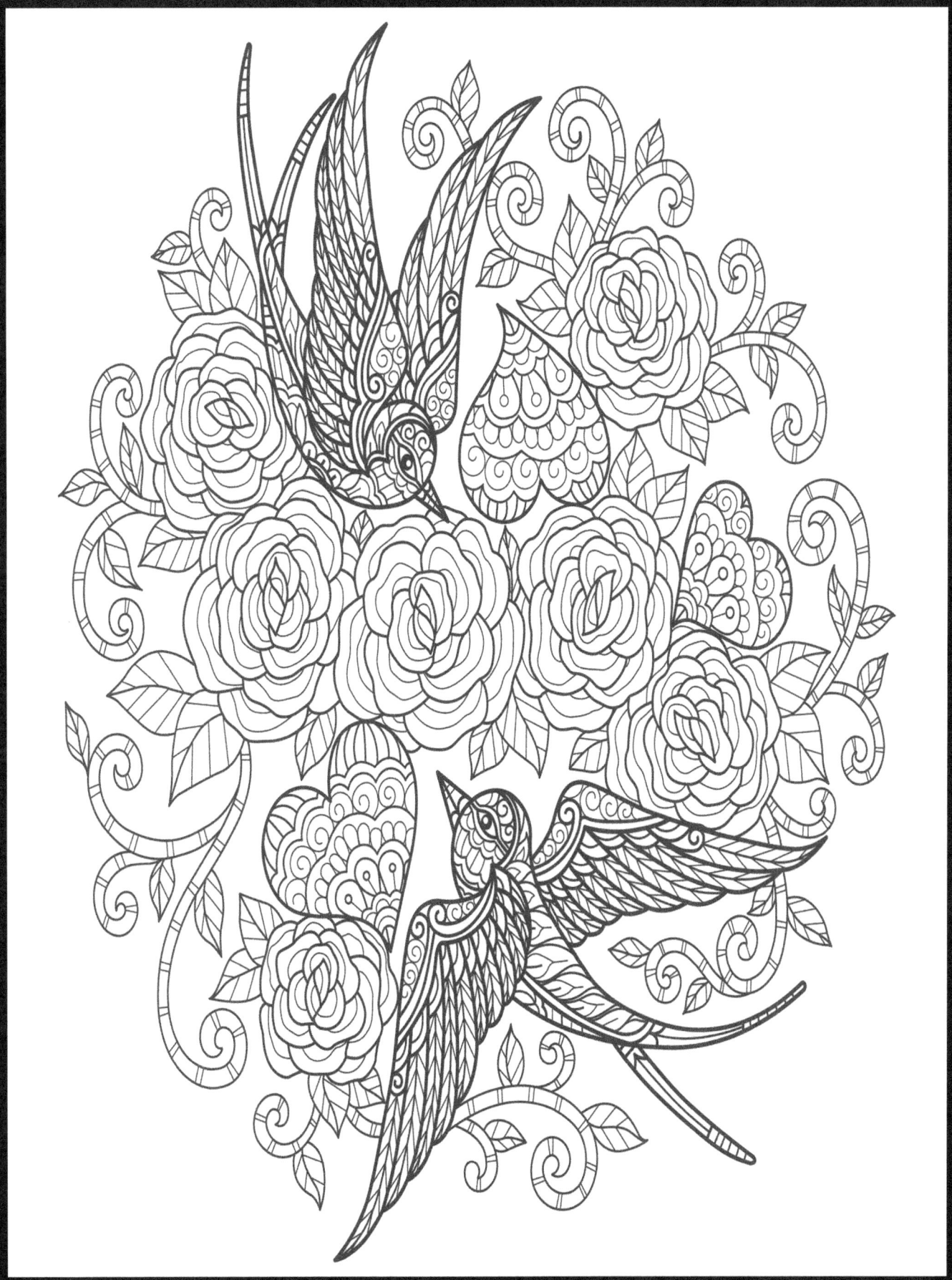

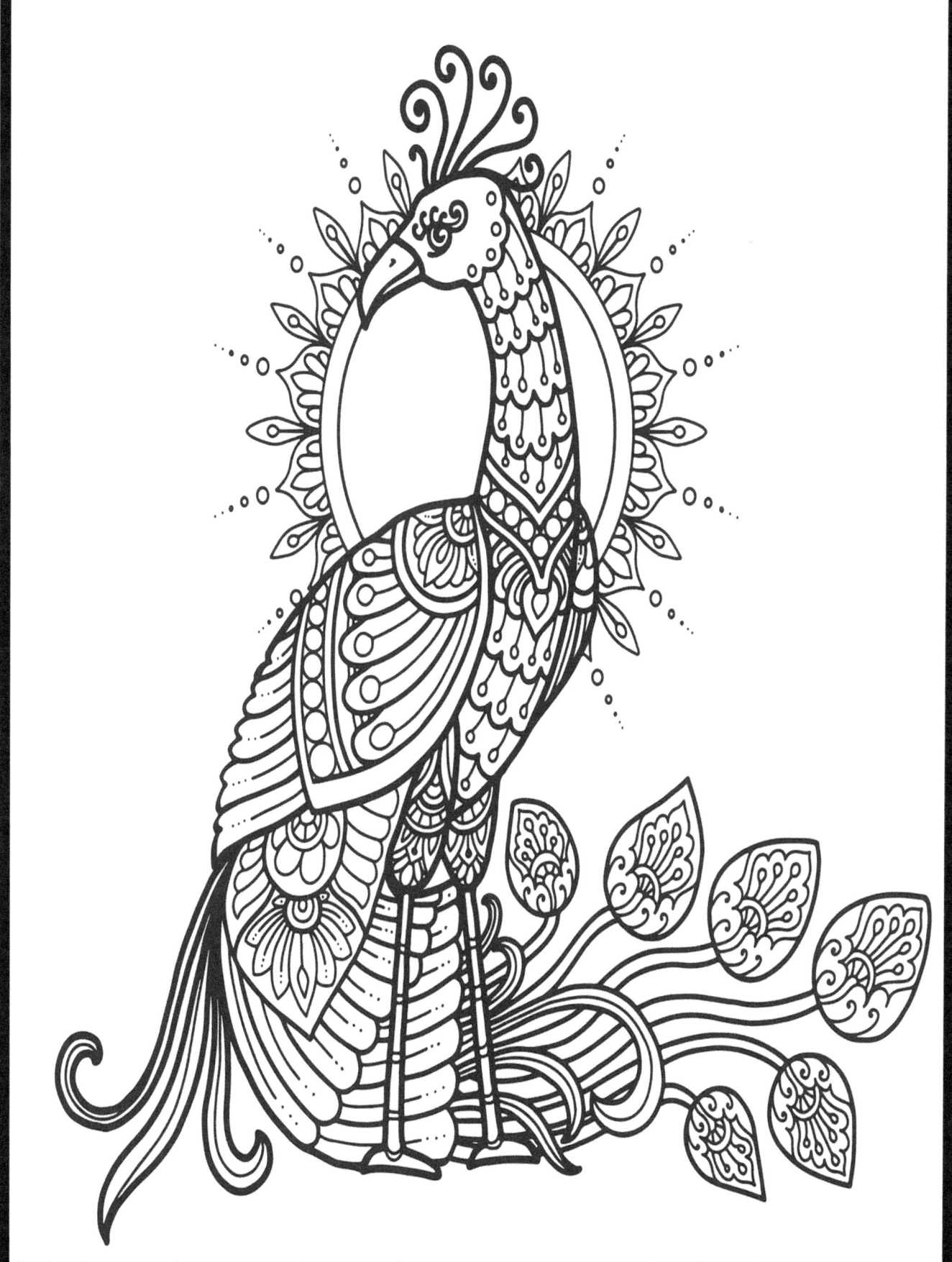

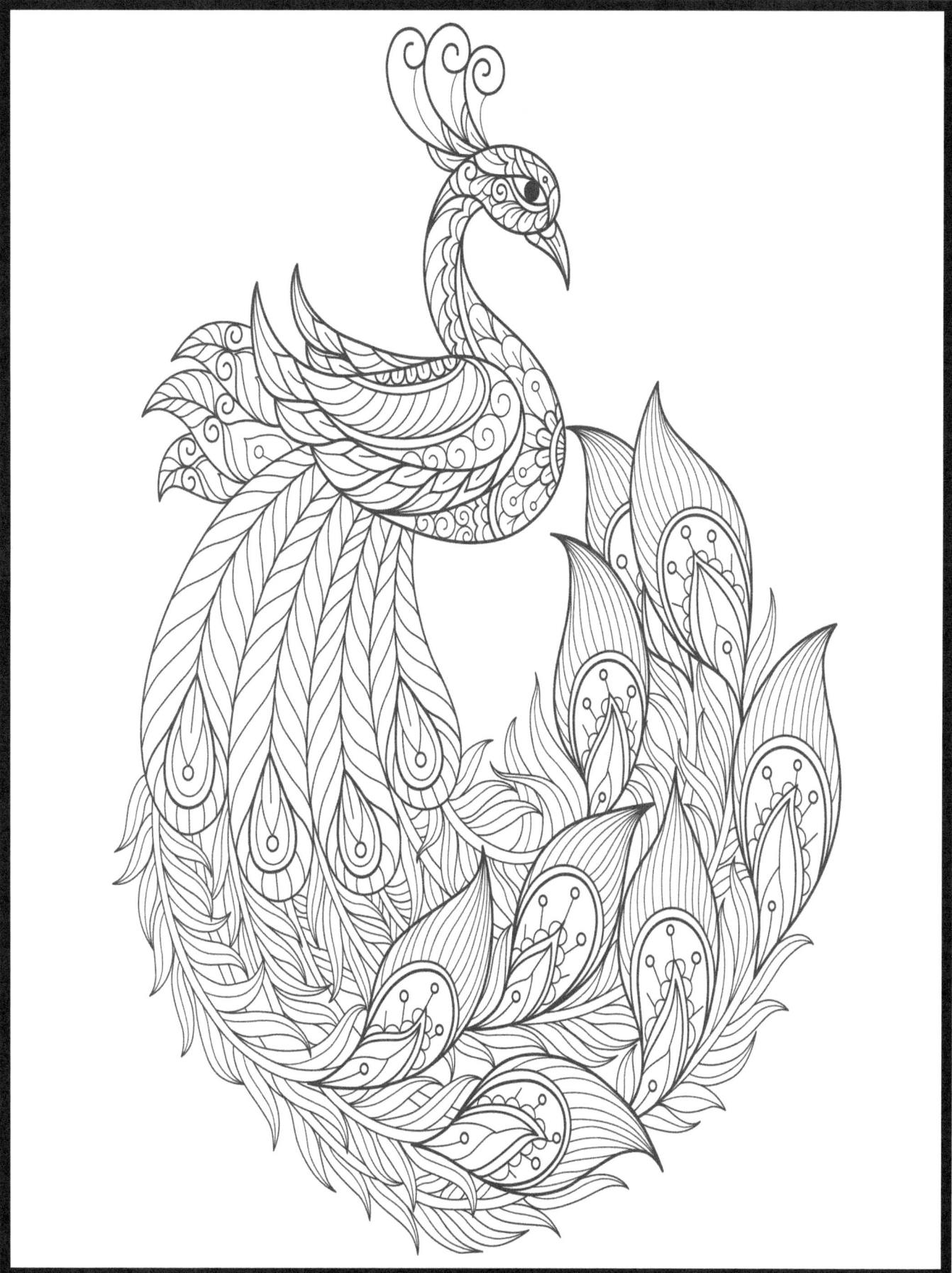

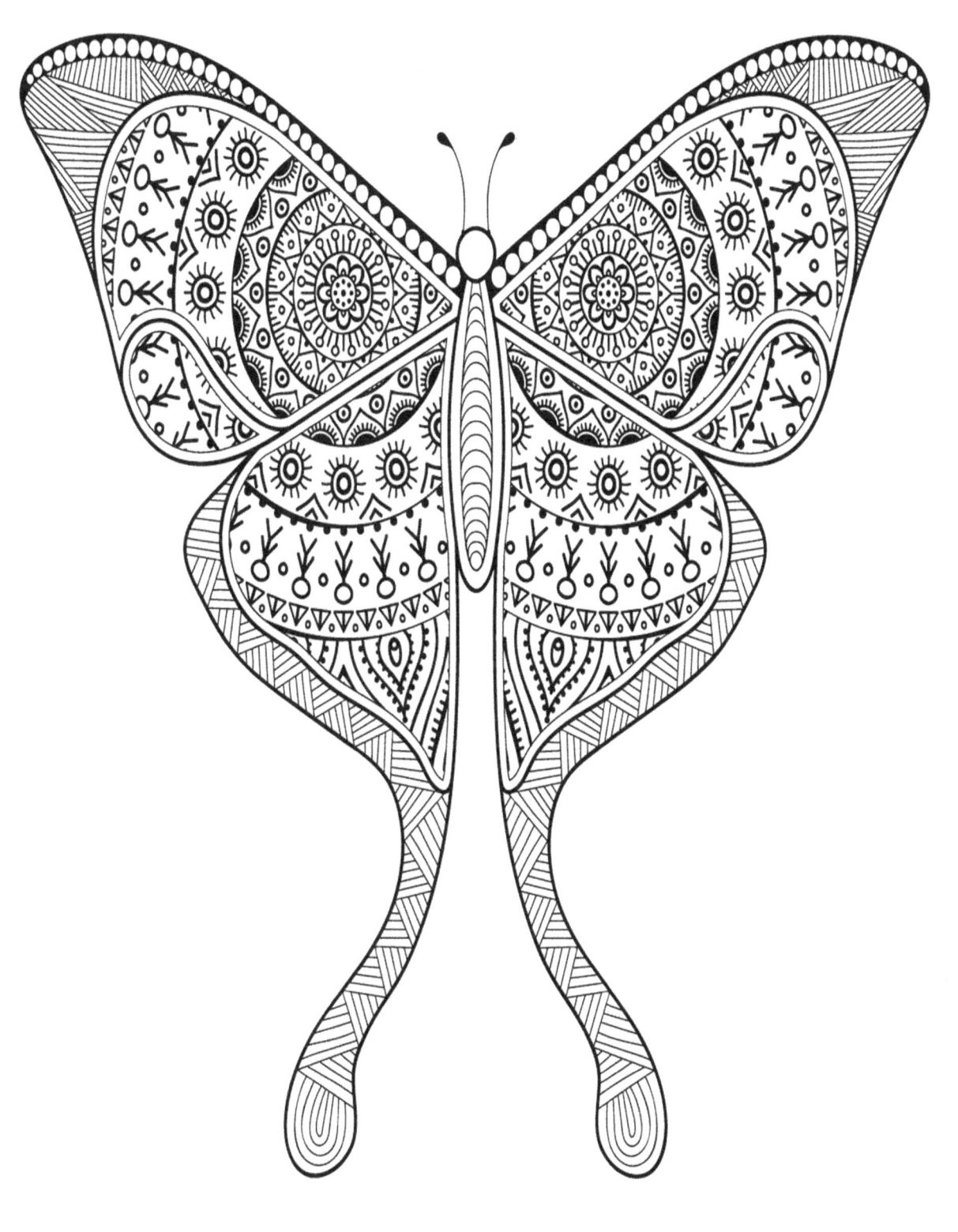

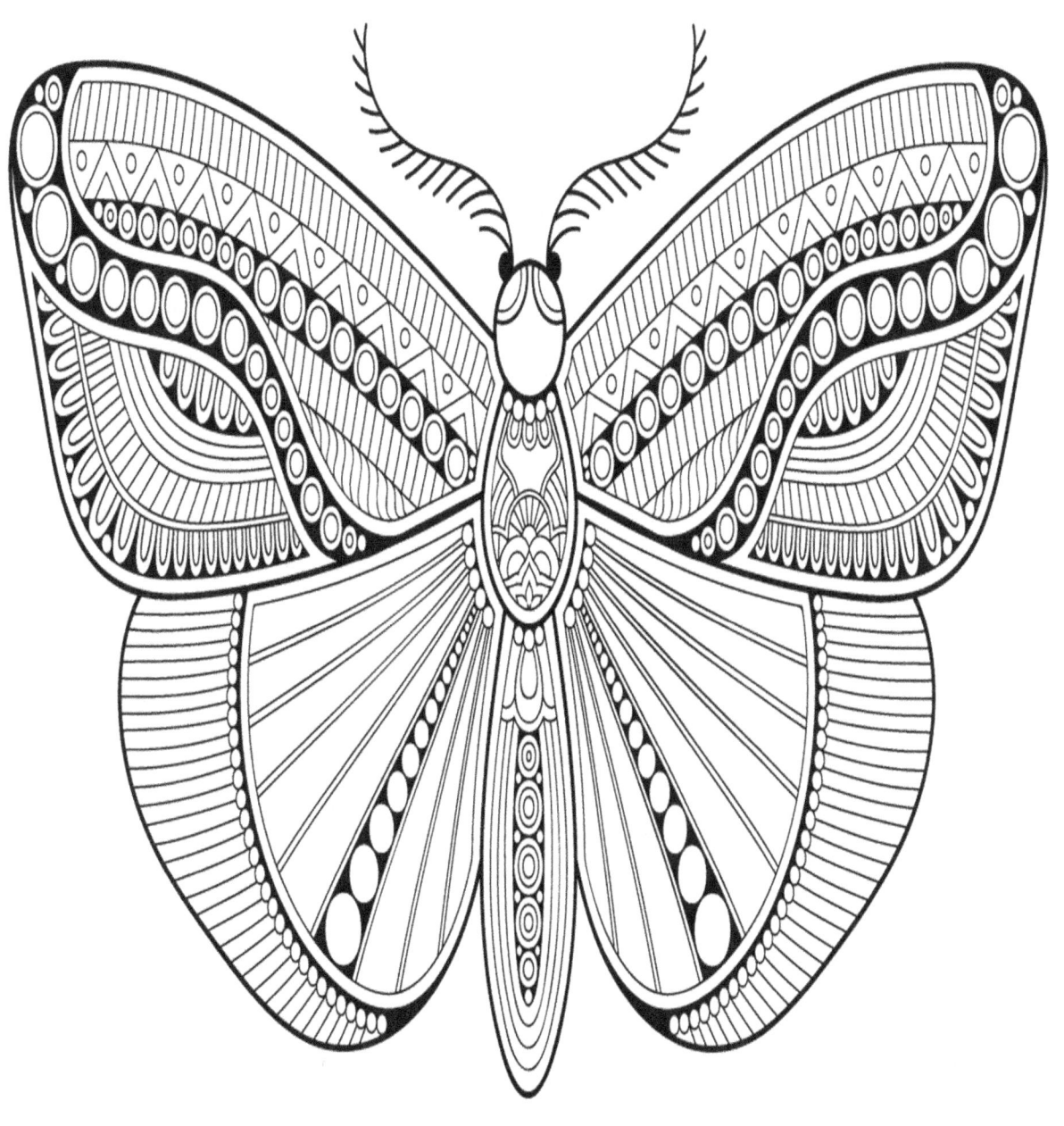

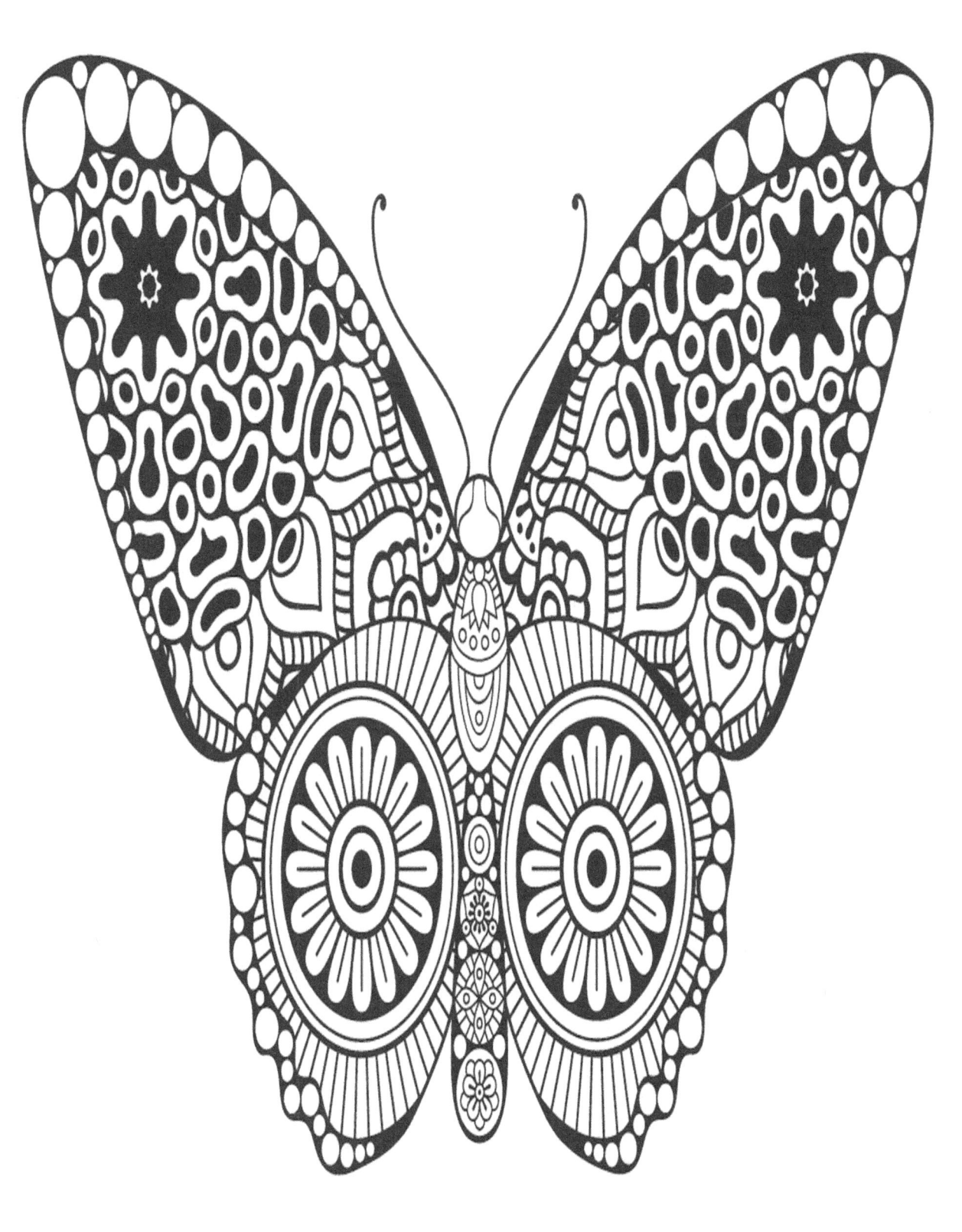

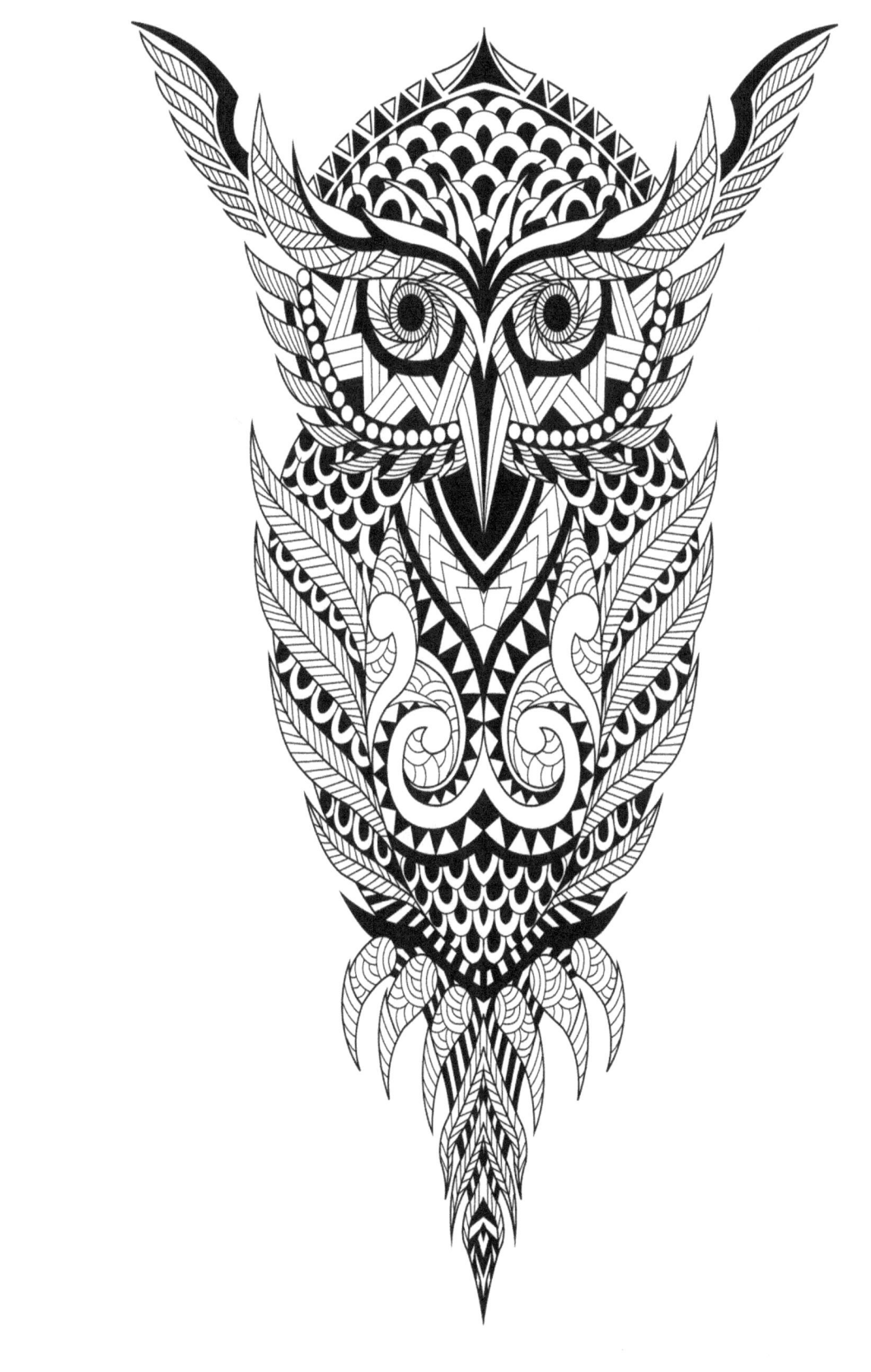

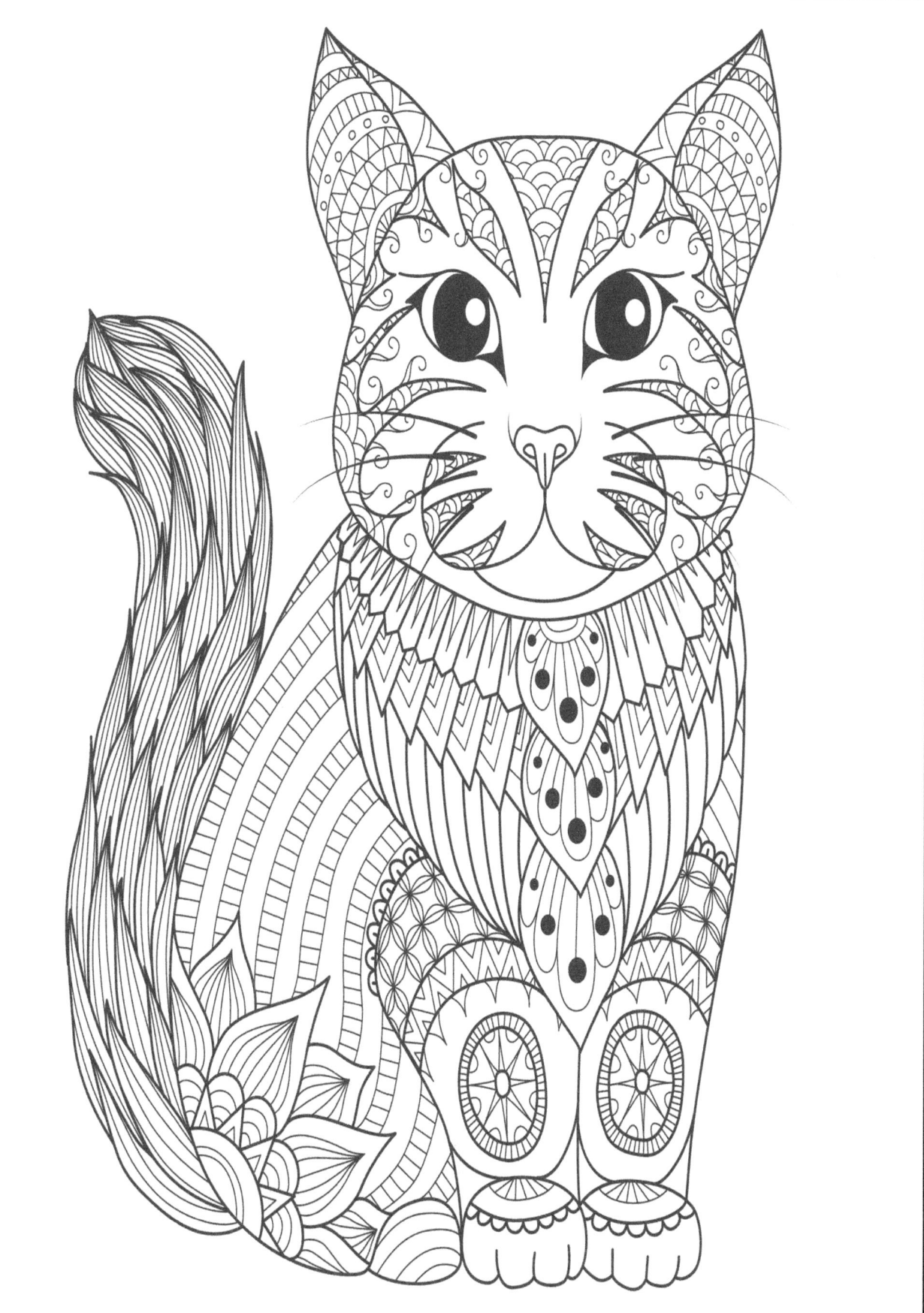

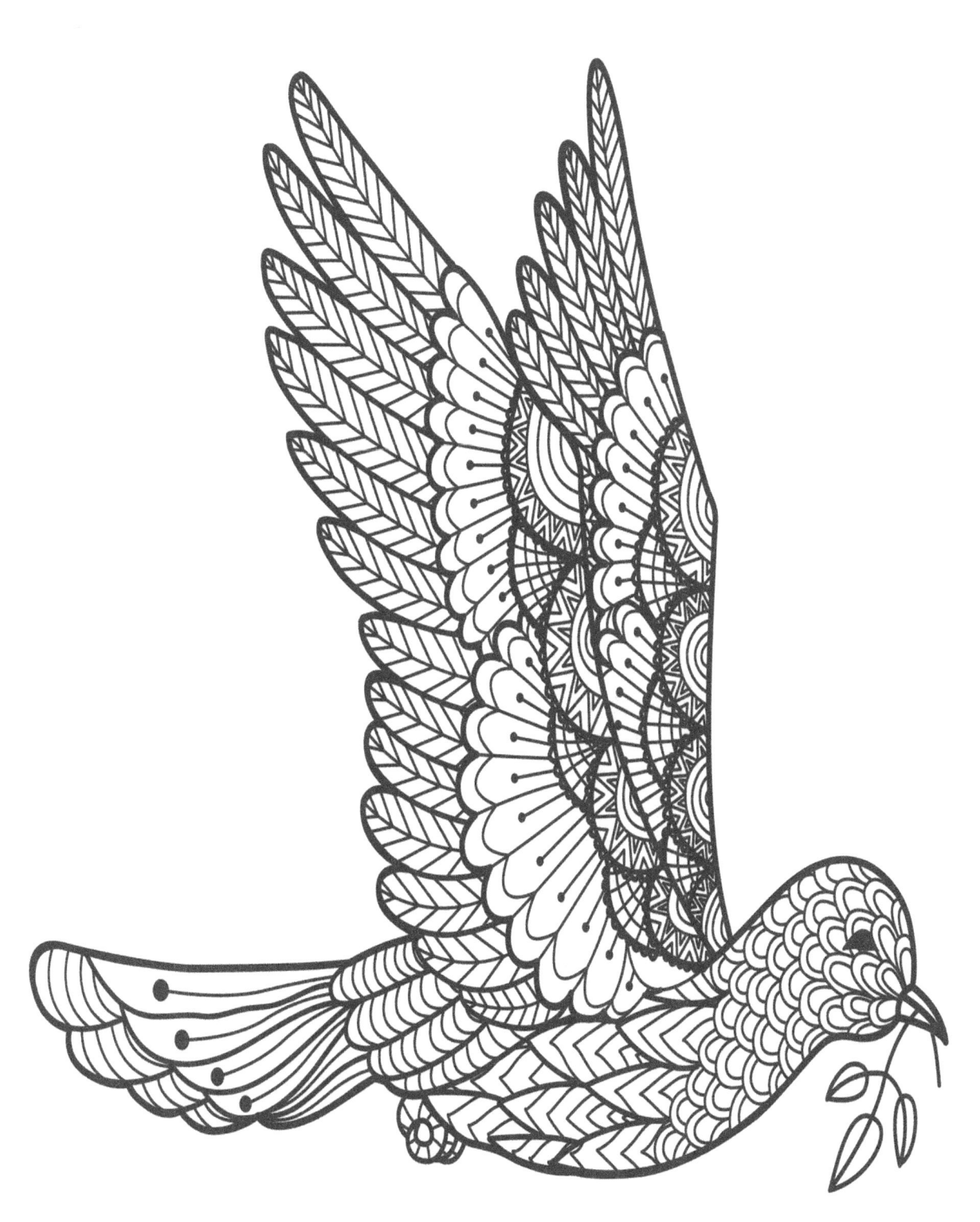

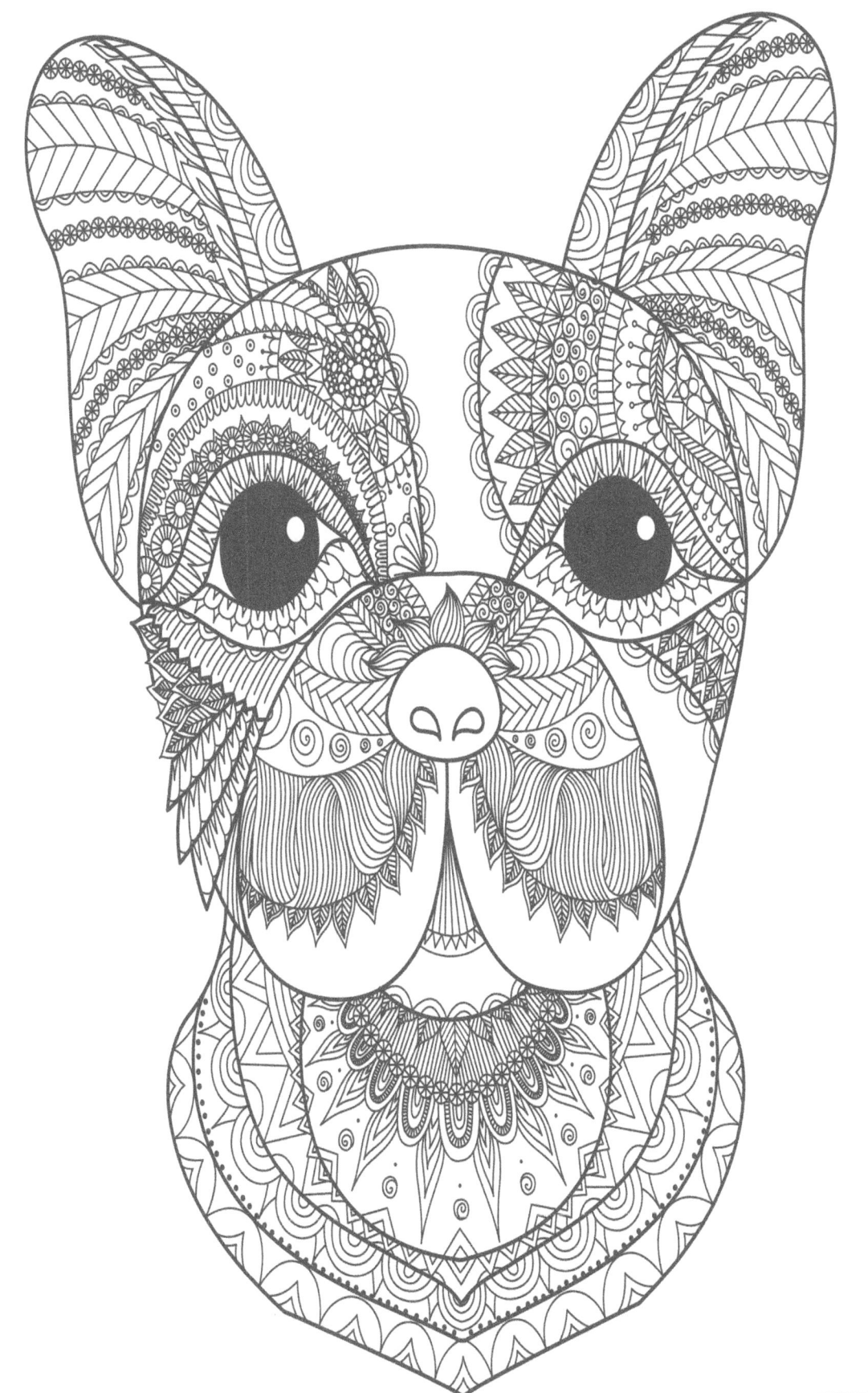

www.ingramcontent.com/pod-product-compliance
Lightning Source LLC
Chambersburg PA
CBHW082018230526
45466CB00022B/2511